JAPAN TRAVEL GUIDE

Traveling Made Easy: Essential Tips, Complete Itineraries and Local Experiences to Discover Unique Places, Culinary Delights and Traditions from North to South for an Unforgettable Journey

Jay Darion & Kaori Miyako

JAY DARION & KAORI MIYAKO

JAPAN TRAVEL GUIDE

ULTIMATE EDITION

Traveling Made Easy: Essential Tips, Complete Itineraries and Local Experiences to Discover Unique Places, Culinary Delights and Traditions from North to South **for an Unforgettable Journey**

TABLE OF CONTENTS

9

INTRODUCTION TO THE ULTIMATE JAPAN TRAVEL GUIDE

Welcome to our ultimate guide to exploring Japan—a land where ancient traditions meet cutting-edge technology, and every corner holds a story waiting to be discovered. As you embark on this journey, imagine yourself stepping into a world where the past and present coexist in harmony, offering experiences that are both awe-inspiring and heartwarming.

Japan is a tapestry of contrasts, where the serene beauty of a Zen garden can be found just a stone's throw away from the bustling energy of a neon-lit cityscape. Whether you're sipping matcha in a centuries-old tea house or navigating the intricate web of Tokyo's subway system, each moment in Japan is an opportunity to engage with a culture that is as rich as it is diverse.

Our guide is designed to be your trusted companion, offering insights and tips that will help you navigate this fascinating country with ease and confidence. We understand that traveling to a place where the language and customs might be unfamiliar can be daunting. But fear not—our aim is to provide you with the tools and knowledge you need to feel at home, whether you're wandering the historic streets of Kyoto or savoring street food in Osaka.

One of the joys of traveling in Japan is the opportunity to experience its distinctive culture firsthand. From the graceful art of the tea ceremony to the vibrant festivals that light up the streets, Japan offers a plethora of cultural experiences that are both immersive and enlightening. We encourage you to embrace these moments, to step out of your comfort zone, and to engage with the people and traditions that make Japan truly unique.

But this guide is not just about what to see and do—it's also about how to do it. We offer practical advice on everything from navigating transportation systems to understanding local etiquette. Our goal is to make your journey as smooth and enjoyable as possible, allowing you to focus on the magic of the experience rather than the logistics.

As you turn the pages of this guide, imagine yourself not just as a tourist, but as a participant in the vibrant tapestry of Japanese life. We hope to inspire you to explore beyond the guidebook, to seek out hidden gems and unexpected adventures that will make your trip unforgettable. Whether you're drawn to the tranquility of a rural onsen or the dynamic pulse of a city that never sleeps, Japan promises a journey of discovery that will leave a lasting impression on your heart.

So, pack your bags, open your mind, and get ready to embark on an adventure like no other. Japan awaits, with its warm hospitality, breathtaking landscapes, and a cultural richness that will captivate your spirit. Welcome to your journey into the heart of Japan.

WELCOME TO JAPAN: ESSENTIAL TRAVEL INFORMATION

As you step off the plane and into the vibrant tapestry of Japan, your senses are immediately awakened. The hum of conversation, the subtle aroma of freshly brewed green tea, and the intricate dance of neon lights against ancient architecture all welcome you. This is a land where the past and future coexist harmoniously, offering a unique blend of experiences that await your discovery.

First, let's address a common concern: the language barrier. While Japanese is the primary language, you'll find that many people, especially in urban areas, have a basic understanding of English. However, learning a few simple phrases like "Arigato" (thank you) or "Sumimasen" (excuse me) can go a long way in showing respect and fostering goodwill.

Transportation in Japan is a marvel in itself. The Shinkansen, or bullet train, is not only a fast and efficient way to travel between cities but also an experience worth savoring. Imagine gliding through the countryside, watching the landscapes shift from bustling cityscapes to serene mountains and rice fields. For tourists, the Japan Rail Pass offers a cost-effective way to explore, providing unlimited travel on most trains, making it an invaluable resource for experiencing Japan's incredible rail network.

A true testament to Japan's transportation innovation is the Maglev (magnetic levitation) train. Using advanced magnetic technology, the Maglev train moves without making contact with the tracks, drastically reducing friction and enabling astonishing speeds over 500 km/h. This futuristic mode of travel is operational in a few select areas, most notably in Japan and China. Japan's Chuo Shinkansen, currently under construction, will eventually connect Tokyo to Nagoya in just 40 minutes, and later extend to Osaka. The combination of Japan's iconic Shinkansen and cutting-edge Maglev technology reflects the country's dedication to both preserving tradition and pushing the boundaries of high-speed rail travel.

Accommodations range from traditional ryokans to modern hotels, each offering a different taste of Japanese hospitality. Staying in a ryokan allows you to experience the tranquility of tatami mats and futons, often accompanied by a soothing soak in an onsen (hot spring).

Finally, immerse yourself in the culture by attending a tea ceremony or exploring local markets. Each interaction, whether it's with a shopkeeper or a fellow traveler, adds a layer to your journey, enriching your understanding of this fascinating country.

• OVERVIEW OF JAPAN'S GEOGRAPHY, HISTORY AND CULTURE

As you embark on your journey across Japan, it's essential to appreciate the intricate tapestry of its geography, history, and culture. Each element intertwines to create the vibrant and dynamic nation that captivates travelers from around the world.

Let's start with Japan's geography. This island nation, nestled in the Pacific Ocean, is composed of four main islands: Honshu, Hokkaido, Kyushu, and Shikoku, along with thousands of smaller islands. The geographical diversity is striking. From the majestic peaks of the Japanese Alps to the serene coastlines of Okinawa, Japan offers landscapes that cater to all kinds of travelers. Whether you're drawn to the bustling cityscapes of Tokyo or the tranquil beauty of rural villages, there's a slice of Japan waiting to be discovered.

Japan's location on the Pacific Ring of Fire means it's prone to natural phenomena like earthquakes and volcanic eruptions. However, these geological features have also blessed the country with stunning natural hot springs, or onsen, which are a must-visit for any traveler seeking relaxation.

Turning to history, Japan's past is as rich and varied as its landscapes. From the ancient Jomon period, which dates back to 14,000 B.C., to the rise of the samurai during the feudal era, Japan's history is marked by periods of isolation and innovation. The influence of the Heian period is particularly noteworthy, as it was a time when art, literature, and culture flourished. This era gave birth to classics like "The Tale of Genji," often considered the world's first novel.

The arrival of the Portuguese in the 16th century marked the beginning of Japan's engagement with the West, leading to the Meiji Restoration in the 19th century, which propelled Japan into the modern age. Understanding these historical shifts is crucial for appreciating the country's contemporary culture and society.

Now, let's delve into the heart of Japan: its culture. Japanese culture is a harmonious blend of tradition and modernity. On one hand, you'll find ancient temples and shrines, such as Kyoto's Kinkaku-ji, where you can feel the echoes of the past. On the other hand, Japan is at the forefront of technology and innovation, exemplified by the neon-lit streets of Akihabara, Tokyo's tech hub.

One of the most endearing aspects of Japanese culture is its emphasis on hospitality, known as omotenashi. This concept goes beyond mere service; it's about anticipating the needs of guests and providing an experience that is both welcoming and memorable. Whether you're staying in a traditional ryokan or a modern hotel, you'll likely encounter this unique approach to hospitality.

Food is another cornerstone of Japanese culture. From the delicate artistry of sushi to the comforting warmth of a bowl of ramen, Japanese cuisine is a journey in itself. Don't miss the chance to try local specialties, such as okonomiyaki in Osaka or fresh seafood in Hokkaido.

Japan is also a land of festivals, each offering a glimpse into the country's cultural fabric. The springtime cherry blossom festivals, or hanami, are a celebration of the fleeting beauty of nature, while autumn brings the vibrant hues of the koyo season. Throughout the year, you'll find festivals that honor everything from the harvest to historical events, each providing a deeper understanding of Japan's cultural heritage.

As you explore Japan, you'll encounter a society that values both tradition and innovation. The juxtaposition of ancient customs with cutting-edge technology creates an environment where the past and present coexist harmoniously. This balance is evident in everyday life, from the meticulous preparation of a traditional tea ceremony to the efficiency of the Shinkansen bullet trains.

In understanding Japan's geography, history, and culture, you'll gain a deeper appreciation for this remarkable country. Whether you're wandering through the historic streets of Kyoto or marveling at the modern architecture of Tokyo, each experience will enrich your journey and leave you with memories that last a lifetime. Embrace the adventure, and let Japan reveal its wonders to you one discovery at a time.

• WHAT TO KNOW BEFORE YOU GO: VISAS, VACCINATIONS, TRAVEL INSURANCE AND USEFUL NUMBERS

Before embarking on your journey to Japan, there are a few essential preparations to ensure your trip is as smooth and enjoyable as possible. Let's start with the practicalities, shall we?

Visas

For many travelers, Japan offers the convenience of a visa exemption for short stays, typically up to 90 days. However, this largely depends on your nationality. It's crucial to check the latest visa requirements well ahead of your departure. The Japanese Ministry of Foreign Affairs website is a reliable resource for this. If you do require a visa, the process is generally straightforward, but it's wise to allow ample time for processing. Remember, having your passport valid for the duration of your stay is a must!

Vaccinations

Japan doesn't require any specific vaccinations for entry, but it's always a good idea to be up-to-date with routine vaccines like measles, mumps, and rubella (MMR), diphtheria-tetanus-pertussis, and influenza. Some travelers opt for the Hepatitis A vaccine, especially if they plan to explore rural areas or indulge in street food. Consult with your healthcare provider about any additional recommendations based on your health history and travel plans.

Travel Insurance

While it might feel like an unnecessary expense, travel insurance is your safety net against unexpected events. From flight cancellations to medical emergencies, having insurance can save you from significant financial strain. Look for a policy that covers health care, especially since medical costs in Japan can be high. Also, consider coverage for trip interruptions or lost luggage. Peace of mind is priceless when you're exploring the wonders of Japan!

Useful Numbers

In an unfamiliar country, having a few key numbers at your fingertips can be reassuring. Here are some you might find handy:

Police: Dial 110 for any emergencies requiring police assistance. Don't worry, they are accustomed to helping tourists and will do their best to assist you.

Ambulance and Fire: Dial 119 for medical emergencies or if you encounter a fire. This number connects you to both ambulance and fire services.

Japan National Tourist Organization (JNTO) Hotline: This 24/7 service can assist with tourist-related inquiries. Dial 050-3816-2787 for English support.

Keep these numbers saved in your phone or written down in a notebook. Trust us, a little preparation goes a long way in ensuring a stress-free journey.

As you finalize these logistical details, remember that they are just the beginning of your adventure. Japan awaits with its breathtaking landscapes, rich traditions, and vibrant cities. With these essentials in place, you're one step closer to a journey that promises to be unforgettable.

(Useful Numbers_continued on page 227)

● CURRENCY EXCHANGE AND TIPPING CUSTOMS

When visiting Japan, it's essential to understand the local currency exchange and tipping practices to enhance your travel experience. The currency used is the Japanese Yen (¥). Before you set out on your trip, take the time to check the current exchange rates. While currency can be exchanged at airports, banks, and hotels, ATMs are often the most convenient and economical choice. Look for ATMs in convenience stores like 7-Eleven or FamilyMart, as they generally accept international cards.

Now, let's discuss tipping—a topic that can be perplexing for many travelers. In Japan, tipping is not a common practice and may even be viewed as disrespectful. The Japanese take immense pride in delivering high-quality service, believing that the act of serving is itself a reward. If you wish to express gratitude for outstanding service, a respectful bow along with a simple "thank you" or "arigatou gozaimasu" is appreciated.

If you feel compelled to give a monetary token of appreciation, there is a culturally appropriate way to do so. Offering a small gift is generally more acceptable. Keep in mind that any cash tip should be placed in an envelope before being given, as handing over money directly is considered rude.

When dining out, it's worth noting that many restaurants include a service charge in the final bill, which removes the necessity for tips. If you're uncertain, don't hesitate to ask, but know that tipping is not expected. By adhering to these customs, you'll avoid awkward situations while showing respect for Japan's rich cultural heritage.

Approach these practices with an open heart and mind, and you'll navigate Japan confidently and respectfully. Enjoy your travels!

• BASIC JAPANESE ETIQUETTE FOR TRAVELERS

As you begin your adventure in Japan, grasping the subtle nuances of Japanese etiquette will enhance your experience and help you earn the respect and warmth of your hosts. Japanese culture places a strong emphasis on respect and politeness, and even a basic understanding of these customs can significantly impact your interactions.

One of the first things to remember is that it is customary to remove your shoes when entering a home or certain traditional establishments. You'll often find slippers available for indoor use. This practice stems from a desire to keep indoor spaces clean and shows respect for your host. Be sure to step directly onto the designated area for shoes when entering to avoid any missteps.

Another vital aspect of Japanese etiquette is bowing. This gesture is a common form of greeting and a means to convey gratitude, apologies, or respect. The angle and duration of the bow can vary based on the context and the individuals involved. For travelers, a slight bow at the waist is usually sufficient and appreciated, signaling your willingness to engage with the culture.

There are several dining customs to keep in mind as well. It is polite to say "Itadakimasu" before you begin your meal, which conveys gratitude for the food and those who prepared it. After finishing your meal, saying "Gochisousama deshita" (thank you for the meal) is also customary. Proper chopstick use is important; avoid placing chopsticks upright in rice or passing food from one pair to another, as these actions resemble funeral practices.

Public behavior in Japan is influenced by a strong sense of harmony and consideration for others. Therefore, keeping noise levels low on public transportation is crucial. Speaking softly on your phone or refraining from calls is a common courtesy. You'll also notice that eating while walking is generally frowned upon; instead, find a designated area to enjoy your snacks or meals.

When it comes to gift-giving, thoughtful gestures can leave a lasting impression. If you're invited to someone's home, bringing a small gift, such as sweets or a souvenir from your country, is a lovely way to express gratitude. Present the gift using both hands as a sign of respect and sincerity.

Lastly, while tipping is prevalent in many cultures, it is not customary in Japan and may even be seen as impolite. Exceptional service is the standard, and Japanese people take pride in their work without expecting extra compensation. A simple thank you and a smile will effectively convey your appreciation.

By incorporating these aspects of Japanese etiquette into your travels, you'll not only move through your journey more smoothly but also gain a richer understanding and appreciation of the culture. Remember, it's often the small gestures that create the most memorable experiences.

NAVIGATING JAPAN: TRANSPORTATION MADE EASY

Picture this: you've just arrived in Japan, the land of the rising sun, and the bustling streets of Tokyo are calling your name. But first, you need to master the art of navigating this incredible country. Fear not, for Japan's transportation system is not only efficient but also an experience in itself.

Let's start with the Shinkansen, or bullet train, a marvel of engineering that whisks you across the country at lightning speed. Imagine watching the countryside blur past your window as you journey from Tokyo to Kyoto in a matter of hours. The Japan Rail Pass is your golden ticket, offering unlimited travel on these trains, perfect for those planning to explore multiple cities.

In the cities, the subway and train networks are your best friends. Tokyo's intricate system might seem daunting at first, but with a bit of practice, you'll be navigating like a local. Signs are in English, and the staff are always willing to help, often with a smile. Don't forget to grab a Suica or Pasmo card for seamless travel on public transport.

For those moments when you prefer a more leisurely pace, consider the charm of local buses, especially in places like Kyoto. These buses meander through historic streets, offering glimpses of traditional Japan. And if you ever feel lost, remember, a simple "Sumimasen" (excuse me) will open doors to friendly assistance.

So, embrace the journey, for in Japan, getting there is half the adventure.

• MASTERING THE JAPAN RAIL PASS (JR PASS) FOR EFFORTLESS TRAVEL

Traveling across Japan is like opening a treasure chest of experiences, and the Japan Rail Pass (JR Pass) is your golden key. This pass is a must-have for anyone looking to explore the country efficiently and affordably. Imagine zipping from the neon-lit streets of Tokyo to the serene temples of Kyoto, all without the hassle of buying individual tickets. The JR Pass offers unlimited travel on most trains operated by the Japan Railways Group, including the famous Shinkansen, or bullet trains.

When it comes to purchasing the JR Pass, timing is everything. It's only available to tourists and must be bought before arriving in Japan. You can purchase it online or through authorized travel agents. Once in Japan, you'll exchange your voucher for the actual pass at a JR office, conveniently located in major airports and stations.

Using the JR Pass is a breeze. Simply show it to the station staff at the manned gates, and you're good to go. For those who like to plan ahead, the pass also allows you to make seat reservations at no extra cost. This can be particularly useful during peak travel seasons or when traveling on popular routes.

One of the JR Pass's greatest benefits is the flexibility it offers. Whether you choose a 7, 14, or 21-day pass, you can tailor your travel to fit your schedule. And while the Shinkansen is a highlight, don't forget that the pass also covers local JR lines, buses, and even some ferries, like the one to Miyajima, home to the iconic floating torii gate.

As you journey through Japan, the JR Pass will not only save you money but also time, allowing you to focus on what truly matters: immersing yourself in the rich tapestry of Japanese culture. With this pass in hand, you're ready to embark on an adventure that's as seamless as it is unforgettable.

• LOCAL TRANSIT: SUBWAYS, BUSES AND TAXIS

As you step into the bustling world of Japan's local transit, a sense of excitement and anticipation fills the air. The intricate web of subways, buses, and taxis is not just a means of transportation but a gateway to the heart of this vibrant country. Navigating these systems can seem daunting at first, but with a little guidance, you'll find yourself moving through Japan with ease and confidence.

The subway is the lifeline of Japan's major cities, connecting neighborhoods with an efficiency that is the envy of the world. In

Tokyo, the Tokyo Metro and Toei Subway systems are your best friends. With color-coded lines and signs in English, you'll quickly find your way around. Remember to purchase a Suica or Pasmo card—these rechargeable cards make travel seamless, allowing you to simply tap and go. And don't worry if you get turned around; the friendly station staff are always eager to help, often with a smile and a few words of English.

Buses, while slightly more challenging due to fewer English signs, offer a unique glimpse into local life, especially in areas where subways don't reach. In cities like Kyoto, buses are often the best way to reach historic sites nestled in the hills.

Pay attention to the fare system, which can vary: in some cities, you pay when you board, while in others, you pay when you alight. A helpful tip is to have small change ready, or better yet, use your Suica or Pasmo card, which is accepted on most buses.

For those moments when you need a more direct route or are simply too tired to navigate public transit, taxis are a reliable option. Japanese taxis are known for their cleanliness and polite drivers. While they can be more expensive, they are a convenient choice, especially late at night or when traveling with heavy luggage. Most taxi drivers speak limited English, so it's wise to have your destination written down in Japanese or show them a map on your phone.

One of the joys of using local transit in Japan is the opportunity to observe and participate in the rhythm of daily life. Whether it's the quiet hum of a subway car during rush hour or the gentle sway of a bus navigating narrow streets, each journey offers a new perspective on the culture and people of Japan.

Embrace the adventure, and soon you'll be navigating like a local, discovering hidden gems and making unforgettable memories along the way.

• RENTING A CAR IN JAPAN: WHEN IT'S WORTH IT AND HOW TO DO IT

Imagine the wind in your hair as you navigate the scenic roads of Japan, discovering hidden temples and serene landscapes far from the bustling crowds. Renting a car in Japan can be a liberating experience, offering a unique way to explore the country at your own pace. However, it's not always the most practical choice, especially in cities like Tokyo where public transport is exceptionally efficient.

When is renting a car worth it? Consider it if you plan to explore rural areas, such as the picturesque countryside of Hokkaido or the quaint villages of the Kiso Valley. These regions offer breathtaking views and cultural experiences that are best accessed by car. Additionally, if you're traveling with family or in a group, having a car can be more economical and comfortable.

To rent a car, you'll need an International Driving Permit (IDP), which you must obtain before arriving in Japan. Once there, major cities and airports have numerous rental agencies like Toyota Rent a Car or Nippon Rent-A-Car. Booking in advance is advisable, especially during peak travel seasons.

Driving in Japan is generally safe, but remember that they drive on the left side of the road. Familiarize yourself with local traffic signs and regulations, and consider renting a GPS with English language support to ease navigation. With these tips, you'll be ready to embark on a memorable road trip through Japan's diverse landscapes.

• PRACTICAL APPS FOR TRANSPORTATION AND NAVIGATION

As you embark on your journey through Japan, you'll find that navigating its intricate web of transportation systems can be both fascinating and bewildering. Thankfully, technology is here to lend a helping hand. One of the most indispensable tools at your disposal is Hyperdia. This app is a lifesaver when it comes to planning train journeys across Japan. By simply entering your starting point and destination, you'll receive detailed schedules, platform information, and even fare costs. It's like having a personal travel assistant in your pocket.

Another essential app is Google Maps. While it might be a familiar tool, its capabilities in Japan are nothing short of extraordinary. It offers real-time updates on public transport, provides walking directions through bustling city streets, and even highlights nearby attractions you might want to explore. Remember to download offline maps before your trip, so you're never left stranded without a signal.

For those moments when you need to communicate with locals or decipher signs, the Google Translate app can be incredibly useful. Its camera feature allows you to translate text instantly, ensuring you can navigate menus and signboards with ease.

With these digital companions, you'll traverse Japan with the confidence of a seasoned traveler, ready to uncover both its famed landmarks and hidden treasures.

WHERE TO STAY: A GUIDE TO ACCOMMODATIONS

Finding the perfect place to stay in Japan is an adventure in itself. Imagine waking up in a traditional ryokan, where tatami mats cushion your step and sliding shoji doors reveal serene garden views. These inns offer a glimpse into Japan's past, often accompanied by a kaiseki meal—a culinary journey through seasonal flavors. For those seeking modern comforts, the bustling heart of Tokyo offers sleek hotels with panoramic cityscapes. Here, you can unwind in a high-tech room, where convenience meets luxury.

For a unique experience, consider staying in a capsule hotel. These compact, futuristic pods are perfect for the solo traveler on a budget, providing a cozy retreat after a day of exploration. If you're traveling with friends or family, renting a traditional machiya house in Kyoto can offer both space and authenticity, allowing you to live like a local.

Regardless of your choice, Japan's hospitality, or omotenashi, ensures a welcoming experience. Embrace the diversity of accommodations, each offering its own story and connection to the culture. Whether it's the quiet elegance of a ryokan or the vibrant energy of a city hotel, your stay will be an integral part of your Japanese journey.

• JAPANESE HOTELS VS. RYOKAN: CHOOSING THE RIGHT EXPERIENCE

Imagine stepping into a world where modernity and tradition coexist in harmony—a place where your accommodation is not just a place to rest, but a doorway into the heart of Japanese culture. Choosing between a Japanese hotel and a Ryokan can shape your journey in profound ways. Let's explore these two distinct experiences, each offering its own unique charm.

Japanese hotels, especially in bustling cities like Tokyo and Osaka, often embrace sleek, contemporary designs. These establishments are equipped with all the conveniences a traveler might expect—high-speed internet, international cuisine, and multilingual staff ready to assist at any hour. For those who prefer a familiar comfort, these hotels offer a seamless blend of Japanese hospitality with global standards. You might find yourself in a room on the 30th floor, gazing out at the neon-drenched cityscape, feeling the pulse of modern Japan beneath you.

However, if your heart yearns for a deeper connection with Japan's rich heritage, a Ryokan might be your ideal choice. Nestled in serene locales, often near hot springs or scenic countryside, Ryokans offer an immersive cultural experience. Imagine sliding open a shoji screen to reveal a meticulously arranged tatami mat room, where simplicity speaks volumes. As you slip into a yukata—a casual kimono—you begin to understand the Japanese art of mindful living. Every element in a Ryokan is designed to promote tranquility and reflection.

One of the highlights of staying at a Ryokan is the opportunity to indulge in a Kaiseki meal, a multi-course dinner that is as much a feast for the eyes as it is for the palate. Each dish is a masterpiece, crafted with seasonal ingredients and served with an attention to detail that reflects centuries of culinary tradition. Sharing this meal in the quiet intimacy of your room or a communal dining area offers a rare glimpse into the culinary artistry that defines Japanese cuisine.

While both accommodations offer unique experiences, they also cater to different aspects of travel. Japanese hotels provide a convenient base for exploring urban attractions, with easy access to public transport and city amenities.

In contrast, a Ryokan stay is an invitation to slow down, to savor the moment, and to connect with the essence of Japan's past. It's about finding peace in the gentle rustle of bamboo or the soothing warmth of an onsen bath.

Ultimately, the choice between a Japanese hotel and a Ryokan depends on what you seek from your journey. Whether you find joy in the vibrant energy of city life or the quiet beauty of traditional settings, both options promise an unforgettable experience in Japan.

Whichever path you choose, remember that each step is a part of your own unique story, waiting to unfold in the enchanting landscape of Japan.

• CAPSULE HOTELS AND BUDGET-FRIENDLY OPTIONS

Imagine stepping into a futuristic cocoon, where space is efficiently maximized, and every detail is designed for your comfort. Welcome to the world of capsule hotels, a uniquely Japanese solution for budget-conscious travelers seeking both convenience and novelty. These compact accommodations are a testament to Japan's ingenuity, offering a practical and affordable option without sacrificing comfort.

Capsule hotels are perfect for those who embrace the minimalist lifestyle. Each capsule is a small, self-contained unit, usually about the size of a single bed, with just enough room to sit up. Despite their size, these capsules are equipped with essential amenities like a comfortable mattress, a personal TV, and power outlets for charging your devices. Privacy is maintained with a curtain or door, allowing you to retreat into your own world after a day of exploration.

One of the most appealing aspects of capsule hotels is their central locations. Often found in bustling city centers, they provide easy access to public transportation, making them an ideal choice for travelers who want to immerse themselves in the urban pulse of cities like Tokyo and Osaka. Imagine waking up in the heart of Shinjuku, stepping out of your capsule, and being just minutes away from iconic attractions like the Tokyo Metropolitan Government Building or the vibrant streets of Kabukicho.

For those concerned about language barriers, capsule hotels offer a reassuringly straightforward experience. Many have multilingual staff and self-check-in kiosks, making the process seamless for non-Japanese speakers. Plus, the communal areas often foster a friendly atmosphere, giving you the chance to meet fellow travelers and share stories over a cup of coffee or a late-night snack from the vending machines.

Beyond capsule hotels, Japan offers a range of budget-friendly accommodations that cater to different tastes and preferences. For a touch of traditional charm, consider staying in a guesthouse or ryokan, where you can experience Japanese hospitality firsthand. These options often include tatami mat rooms and communal baths, providing a glimpse into the country's rich cultural heritage.

Hostels are another excellent choice for budget travelers, especially those who enjoy a social environment. Many hostels in Japan are designed with modern travelers in mind, offering chic interiors, shared kitchens, and even organized events like city tours or cooking classes. Whether you're traveling solo or with friends, hostels can be a great way to connect with like-minded adventurers.

In Japan, budget travel doesn't mean compromising on quality. Whether you choose a capsule hotel, guesthouse, or hostel, you'll find that each option offers its own unique charm, ensuring that your journey is both affordable and memorable. So pack your bags, embrace the adventure, and rest easy knowing that a comfortable and budget-friendly stay awaits you in the Land of the Rising Sun.

• AIRBNB AND ALTERNATIVE STAYS: HOW THEY WORK IN JAPAN

When it comes to exploring Japan, finding the right place to stay can truly enhance your experience. While hotels are a classic choice, many travelers are now opting for Airbnb and alternative accommodations to dive deeper into local life. These options not only offer a unique taste of Japanese culture but also provide a more personal and often more affordable experience.

In Japan, Airbnb has become increasingly popular, especially in bustling cities like Tokyo and Kyoto. Staying at an Airbnb can give you a sense of what it's like to live in Japan, with accommodations ranging from modern apartments to traditional houses. Many hosts are eager to share their local knowledge, offering tips on hidden gems and must-see spots that you might not find in a typical guidebook. This personal touch can be invaluable, helping you navigate the nuances of Japanese culture with ease.

It's important to note that Japan has specific regulations regarding short-term rentals. Hosts must register their properties and display a registration number, ensuring that your stay is both legal and safe. When booking, make sure the listing includes this information. This attention to detail reflects Japan's commitment to quality and hospitality, providing peace of mind during your travels.

Beyond Airbnb, there are other alternative stays that can enrich your journey. Consider a stay at a ryokan, a traditional Japanese inn. These establishments offer a glimpse into Japan's rich history and customs, often featuring tatami-matted rooms, futon bedding, and communal baths. Ryokans are typically found in scenic areas, making them perfect for those looking to escape the hustle and bustle of city life and immerse themselves in nature.

For the more adventurous, a temple stay can be a transformative experience. Many temples across Japan open their doors to guests, allowing you to participate in meditation sessions, experience vegetarian Buddhist cuisine, and enjoy the tranquility of temple grounds. This is a unique opportunity to connect with Japan's spiritual heritage and find inner peace amidst your travels.

Remember, no matter where you choose to stay, the key is to embrace the experience fully. Whether you're sipping tea in a cozy Airbnb, enjoying a kaiseki meal at a ryokan, or waking up to the sound of temple bells, these moments will become cherished memories of your journey through Japan. So, approach each stay with an open heart and a curious mind, ready to discover the soul of this incredible country.

● TIPS FOR BOOKING ACCOMMODATIONS AND AVOIDING COMMON MISTAKES

When it comes to booking accommodations in Japan, the landscape is as diverse as the country itself, offering everything from traditional ryokans to modern capsule hotels. To ensure a smooth experience, start by considering the location. Proximity to public transportation is crucial, especially in cities like Tokyo and Osaka, where the train system is your best friend. Staying near a station can save you valuable time and energy.

Next, think about the type of lodging that suits your travel style. If you're seeking an authentic experience, consider a stay at a ryokan, where you can enjoy tatami mats and kaiseki meals. For budget travelers, capsule hotels offer a unique and economical option, though they might not be ideal for those who are claustrophobic.

Booking in advance is generally advisable, particularly during peak seasons like cherry blossom and autumn leaf viewing. Use reliable platforms such as Booking.com or Rakuten Travel, which often provide user reviews and detailed descriptions. However, don't overlook the potential for hidden gems; smaller inns and guesthouses can offer a more personal touch and insight into local life.

When browsing options, pay attention to the amenities offered. Many accommodations offer free Wi-Fi, but double-check if you need it for work or planning your daily adventures. Also, be aware of the check-in and check-out times, as some places have strict policies that can catch travelers off guard.

Finally, communicate any special requests or needs in advance. Most Japanese accommodations are hospitable and willing to accommodate dietary restrictions or accessibility needs if informed early. By following these tips, you can avoid common pitfalls and enjoy a worry-free stay in Japan, leaving you to focus on the incredible experiences awaiting you outside your door.

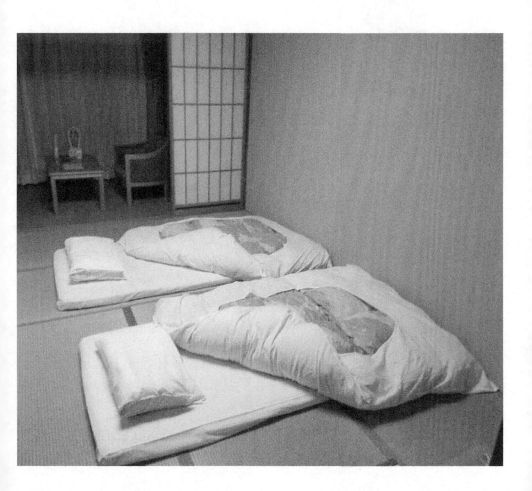

FOOD CULTURE: EATING LIKE A LOCAL

Imagine stepping into a bustling izakaya, the air filled with the savory aroma of grilled yakitori and the cheerful clinking of glasses. Here, in the heart of Japan's vibrant food scene, is where one truly eats like a local. The journey begins as you slide open the wooden door, greeted by a chorus of "Irasshaimase!" from the staff. It's a warm welcome into the world of Japanese culinary delights, where tradition meets modernity in every bite.

Dining in Japan is not just about the food; it's an experience. Picture yourself at a sushi counter, watching a master chef deftly slice fresh fish with the precision of a samurai. Each piece of sushi is a work of art, a testament to years of dedication and respect for the craft. You'll find that the best sushi is not always in high-end restaurants but often in the unassuming corners of local markets, where the freshest catches are served with a smile.

For the adventurous, street food offers a treasure trove of flavors. From the sizzling takoyaki stalls of Osaka to the delicate taiyaki in Tokyo, these bites tell stories of the regions they hail from. And don't miss the chance to try a bowl of steaming ramen, where each slurp reveals a new layer of flavor, crafted with love and care.

Embark on this culinary journey with an open heart and an empty stomach. Remember, the essence of eating like a local in Japan is not just about the food itself but the shared moments, the laughter, and the stories that unfold with every meal.

• Traditional Japanese meals: Sushi, ramen, Yakitori and more

Imagine sitting at a quaint, wooden counter, the aroma of vinegared rice mingling with the salty breeze of the nearby sea. This is the essence of enjoying sushi in Japan. Each piece is a work of art, crafted meticulously by the hands of a seasoned sushi chef. The fish, often caught fresh from local waters, melts in your mouth, a symphony of flavors that speaks of the ocean's bounty. For an authentic experience, try the omakase style, where the chef selects the best offerings of the day, guiding you through a culinary journey that is both intimate and unforgettable.

Yet, Japan's culinary landscape is vast and varied. From the bustling streets of Tokyo to the serene temples of Kyoto, you'll find ramen shops tucked away like hidden treasures. Each region boasts its own version, whether it's the rich, pork-based broth of Tonkotsu from Fukuoka or the soy-flavored Shoyu ramen of Tokyo. Slurping is not only allowed but encouraged, a sign of appreciation for the chef's labor of love. As you savor each mouthful, you'll discover that ramen is not just a meal but a comforting embrace, especially on a chilly evening.

For those who enjoy a more interactive dining experience, yakitori offers a delightful option. These skewered morsels of grilled chicken, seasoned with salt or a savory tare sauce, are perfect for pairing with a cold beer or sake. Gathered around a bustling yakitori stall, you'll find locals and travelers alike, sharing stories and laughter over these bite-sized delights. It's a social affair, a chance to connect with the heart of Japanese culture while indulging in its flavors.

Of course, no exploration of Japanese cuisine would be complete without mentioning the delicate art of kaiseki. This traditional multi-course meal is a feast for the senses, where each dish is presented with an eye for detail and a respect for seasonal ingredients. From the subtle flavors of a clear soup to the vibrant colors of pickled vegetables, kaiseki is a celebration of balance and harmony, reflecting the natural beauty of Japan itself.

As you journey through Japan, let these traditional meals be your guide, offering not just sustenance but a deeper understanding of the culture and its people. Each bite tells a story, a narrative of tradition, innovation, and the timeless connection between food and community.

• NAVIGATING FOOD MENUS AND ORDERING LIKE A PRO

Picture this: you're seated in a cozy izakaya, the soft hum of conversation around you, the tantalizing aroma of grilled yakitori wafting through the air. The menu, however, is a mystery, filled with kanji and hiragana that seem to dance across the page. Fear not, dear traveler, for navigating Japanese food menus and ordering like a pro can be an adventure in itself, and we're here to guide you every step of the way.

First, let's tackle the menu. In many restaurants, you'll find menus with pictures, which can be a great help. Don't be afraid to point to what looks good. The staff are usually very understanding and eager to assist. If you're lucky, you might encounter menus with English translations, especially in tourist-friendly areas like Tokyo and Kyoto. However, for a truly authentic experience, venturing into local spots with Japanese-only menus can be incredibly rewarding.

Understanding a few key Japanese words can make all the difference. For instance, knowing that "tori" means chicken, "sake" refers to salmon, and "gyoza" are delicious dumplings can help you identify dishes you might enjoy. If you're adventurous, try ordering the "omakase" option, which means leaving it up to the chef to surprise you with their best offerings.

When it comes to ordering, a little politeness goes a long way. Begin with a friendly "sumimasen" (excuse me) to get the attention of the staff. You can then use "kudasai" to politely request your dish. For example, "Sushi o kudasai" means "Sushi, please." If you have dietary restrictions or preferences, phrases like "niku nashi" (no meat) or "yasai dake" (only vegetables) can be useful.

Don't be surprised if your meal is accompanied by a chorus of "arigatou gozaimasu" (thank you very much) from the staff. It's a lovely custom that adds to the warm hospitality you'll find throughout Japan.

Finally, savor the experience. Each dish is a story, a piece of Japan's rich culinary tapestry. From the delicate flavors of sashimi to the hearty warmth of ramen, let your taste buds embark on their own journey. With a bit of courage and curiosity, you'll soon find yourself ordering with ease and enjoying every bite of your Japanese culinary adventure.

• DIETARY CONSIDERATIONS: VEGETARIAN, VEGAN, AND GLUTEN-FREE OPTIONS

When embarking on a culinary journey through Japan, it's essential to consider dietary preferences and restrictions. Whether you're a vegetarian, vegan, or require gluten-free options, Japan offers a plethora of choices that ensure you won't miss out on the country's rich flavors and culinary traditions.

For vegetarians, Japan is a treasure trove of plant-based delights. While traditional Japanese cuisine often centers around seafood and meat, there are numerous dishes that cater to vegetarian tastes. Dishes like tempura (lightly battered and fried vegetables) and zaru soba (cold buckwheat noodles served with a dipping sauce) are not only delicious but also widely available. Don't miss out on shōjin ryōri, the traditional Buddhist temple cuisine that is entirely vegetarian and offers a serene dining experience.

Vegans may face a bit more of a challenge, as many Japanese dishes use fish-based broths or seasonings. However, with a bit of preparation, you can savor Japan's culinary offerings without compromising your lifestyle. Look for restaurants that specialize in shōjin ryōri, as these establishments often cater to vegans. Also, consider visiting macrobiotic cafes, which are gaining popularity in urban areas like Tokyo and Kyoto. Be sure to learn a few key phrases in Japanese to communicate your dietary needs, such as asking if a dish contains katsuobushi (bonito flakes) or dashi (fish broth).

For those seeking gluten-free options, Japan's reliance on soy sauce and wheat-based noodles can be daunting. However, you can still enjoy a gluten-free culinary adventure with some mindful choices. Opt for rice-based dishes like sushi or onigiri (rice balls) and avoid soy sauce, unless it's specifically labeled gluten-free. Explore the world of sashimi for a fresh, gluten-free experience, and don't forget to try mochi, a delightful gluten-free dessert made from glutinous rice.

As you navigate Japan's culinary landscape, remember that many restaurants are becoming increasingly aware of dietary needs and are more than willing to accommodate. With a spirit of adventure and a little research, you can enjoy a fulfilling and inclusive dining experience across the Land of the Rising Sun.

• MUST-VISIT FOOD MARKETS AND STREET FOOD HOTSPOTS

As you wander through the vibrant streets of Japan, your senses are bound to be captivated by the tantalizing aromas wafting from bustling food markets and street food stalls. These culinary hotspots are not just places to grab a quick bite, but gateways to understanding the country's rich culinary heritage and diverse flavors.

Let's start with Tsukiji Outer Market in Tokyo, a paradise for seafood lovers. While the inner wholesale market has moved to Toyosu, the outer market remains a lively hub where you can sample fresh sushi, grilled shellfish, and other seafood delicacies. Strolling through the narrow alleys, you'll encounter vendors offering everything from tamago-yaki (sweet rolled omelet) to uni (sea urchin) atop rice bowls. The market's bustling energy and the vendors' enthusiastic calls create an atmosphere that's both exhilarating and inviting.

In Osaka, known as Japan's kitchen, the Kuromon Ichiba Market is a must-visit. This market offers a feast for both the eyes and the palate, with colorful displays of fresh produce, meats, and seafood. Here, you can indulge in takoyaki (octopus balls), a beloved Osaka street food, or savor the rich flavors of kushikatsu (deep-fried skewers). As you navigate the market, don't hesitate to engage with the friendly vendors who are always eager to share their passion for food and offer cooking tips.

Kyoto's Nishiki Market is another gem, offering a glimpse into the city's culinary traditions. Known as "Kyoto's Kitchen," this market is a treasure trove of local specialties.

Try yuba (tofu skin), a delicacy unique to the region, or pick up some matcha (green tea) treats to enjoy later. The market's narrow lanes are filled with the chatter of locals and tourists alike, creating a warm and welcoming atmosphere that invites exploration.

For those seeking a more off-the-beaten-path experience, the Omicho Market in Kanazawa offers a taste of the Sea of Japan's bounty. This market is renowned for its fresh seafood, particularly the succulent kani (crab) and ama-ebi (sweet shrimp). Wander through the stalls and sample some grilled fish or enjoy a steaming bowl of kaisen-don (seafood rice bowl) as you soak in the local atmosphere.

No journey through Japan's street food scene would be complete without a visit to the vibrant street food stalls of Fukuoka. Known as yatai, these open-air food stalls line the streets, offering a casual dining experience. Here, you can savor Hakata ramen, famous for its rich pork broth and thin noodles, or try motsunabe, a hearty hot pot dish. The convivial atmosphere of the yatai, with patrons sharing tables and stories, provides a unique opportunity to connect with locals and fellow travelers.

As you explore these culinary havens, remember that food in Japan is more than just sustenance; it's an expression of culture, history, and regional identity. Each bite tells a story, inviting you to delve deeper into the heart of Japan. So, embrace the adventure, savor the flavors, and let Japan's food markets and street food hotspots guide you on a delicious journey.

TOP CITIES TO VISIT: HIGHLIGHTS AND HIDDEN GEMS

Embarking on a journey through Japan's top cities offers a kaleidoscope of experiences, each with its own rhythm and charm. Tokyo, the vibrant heart of Japan, pulsates with energy. From the neon-lit streets of Shibuya to the serene gardens of the Imperial Palace, Tokyo is a city of contrasts. Let yourself be swept away by the organized chaos of its subway system, a marvel of efficiency, as you explore hidden izakayas and savor the delicate flavors of sushi crafted by masters.

In Kyoto, time seems to slow down. The city whispers tales of ancient Japan, with its tranquil temples and traditional tea houses. Stroll through the Arashiyama Bamboo Grove, where towering stalks sway gently in the breeze, creating a natural symphony. Here, the art of the tea ceremony is not just a tradition but a passage into the soul of Japan. Don't miss the chance to wear a kimono and walk the cobblestone streets of Gion, where you might catch a glimpse of a geisha.

Osaka, known for its culinary delights, invites you to indulge in street food adventures. From takoyaki to okonomiyaki, the flavors are bold and unforgettable. The locals, with their warm and boisterous nature, will make you feel at home. Discover the city's hidden gems, like the retro charm of Shinsekai or the neon wonderland of Dotonbori, where the iconic Glico Man beckons.

Beyond these well-trodden paths, Japan is a treasure trove of hidden gems. Venture to the quiet town of Kanazawa, where traditional crafts like gold leafing and silk dyeing thrive. Or perhaps, the island of Naoshima, a haven for contemporary art lovers, where art installations blend seamlessly with the landscape. Each city, each corner of Japan, offers a unique story, waiting to be discovered.

● TOKYO: BEYOND THE SKYSCRAPERS AND INTO THE NEIGHBORHOODS

When most people think of Tokyo, they envision a sprawling metropolis dominated by towering skyscrapers and the frenetic pace of city life. However, beyond the glitzy facades and neon-lit streets lies a tapestry of vibrant neighborhoods each with its own unique charm and character. These areas offer a glimpse into the soul of Tokyo, where tradition and modernity coexist in a delicate balance.

Let's start with Yanaka, a neighborhood that feels like a step back in time. Known for its narrow alleyways and old wooden houses, Yanaka survived the bombings of World War II and the rapid modernization that followed. As you stroll through its quiet streets, you'll discover a plethora of small temples, traditional craft shops, and quaint cafes. Be sure to visit the Yanaka Cemetery, a peaceful oasis that's home to the graves of many famous Japanese figures, including the last shogun of the Edo period.

Another gem is Shimokitazawa, a bohemian enclave teeming with vintage shops, live music venues, and quirky cafes. It's a haven for Tokyo's creative crowd, where you can spend hours browsing through second-hand bookstores or enjoying a coffee in a cozy nook. The neighborhood's laid-back vibe is a refreshing contrast to the hustle and bustle of the city center, making it a perfect spot to unwind and soak up the local culture.

For those interested in Tokyo's culinary scene, the neighborhood of Tsukiji is a must-visit. While the famous fish market has moved to Toyosu, the outer market remains a bustling hub of activity, offering a mouth-watering array of fresh seafood and local delicacies. Wander through the lively stalls, sample some grilled eel or tamagoyaki, and experience the vibrant energy that defines Tokyo's food culture. Don't miss the chance to try a sushi breakfast at one of the market's many small eateries, where the fish is as fresh as it gets.

In contrast, the neighborhood of Kagurazaka offers a taste of old-world elegance. Once a thriving geisha district, Kagurazaka is now known for its charming cobblestone streets and a mix of traditional and modern establishments. Here, you'll find a delightful blend of French and Japanese influences, with patisseries nestled alongside kaiseki restaurants. Take a leisurely stroll down the main street, and you'll uncover hidden gems like small shrines and cozy izakayas, where you can enjoy an evening of sake and small plates.

Finally, no exploration of Tokyo's neighborhoods would be complete without a visit to Asakusa. Home to the iconic Senso-ji Temple, Tokyo's oldest temple, Asakusa is steeped in history and culture. As you approach the temple, you'll pass through the bustling Nakamise Shopping Street, lined with stalls selling traditional snacks and souvenirs. Once inside the temple grounds, take a moment to admire the stunning architecture and soak in the spiritual atmosphere. Asakusa offers a perfect blend of the old and new, with traditional rickshaws sharing the streets with modern skyscrapers in the distance.

Exploring these neighborhoods allows you to peel back the layers of Tokyo and discover the authentic heart of the city. Each area offers a different perspective, weaving together the stories of Tokyo's past and present. Whether you're a history buff, a foodie, or simply a curious traveler, these neighborhoods promise a deeper connection to Japan's vibrant capital, inviting you to experience the city's rich tapestry of life beyond its iconic skyline.

• KYOTO: TEMPLES, TEA HOUSES AND TRADITIONAL CRAFTS

Kyoto, a city where ancient traditions harmoniously blend with the modern world, is a place where you can truly experience the essence of Japan. As you wander through its streets, you'll find yourself surrounded by the serene beauty of temples, the delicate artistry of traditional crafts, and the calming atmosphere of tea houses. Kyoto is not just a destination; it's a journey into the heart of Japanese culture.

Begin your exploration with a visit to the iconic Kinkaku-ji, the Golden Pavilion. This stunning Zen temple, covered in brilliant gold leaf, is a sight that captures the imagination. As you stroll through its meticulously maintained gardens, take a moment to reflect by the mirror-like pond that perfectly reflects the temple's grandeur. It's a place that invites contemplation and offers a glimpse into the spiritual heritage of Japan.

Next, make your way to the Arashiyama Bamboo Grove, a magical place that feels like stepping into another world. The towering bamboo stalks sway gently in the breeze, creating a natural symphony that soothes the soul. As you walk along the path, you'll feel a sense of tranquility that is hard to find elsewhere. This is a perfect spot to pause and appreciate the natural beauty that Kyoto has to offer.

No visit to Kyoto would be complete without experiencing a traditional tea ceremony. Head to one of the city's charming tea houses, where you can witness the art of tea preparation, a practice steeped in history and ritual. The serene environment, coupled with the rich flavors of matcha, provides a moment of peace and reflection. It's an opportunity to connect with the cultural traditions that have been passed down through generations.

For those interested in traditional crafts, Kyoto offers a wealth of opportunities to explore the artistic heritage of Japan. Visit the workshops of skilled artisans who create beautiful textiles, ceramics, and paper crafts. In the Nishijin district, you can watch the intricate process of weaving kimono fabrics, a craft that has been perfected over centuries. These experiences not only showcase the skill and dedication of the craftsmen but also allow you to take home a piece of Kyoto's cultural legacy.

As you continue your journey, be sure to explore the narrow streets of the Gion district, famous for its traditional wooden machiya houses and as the home of Kyoto's geisha culture. Strolling through Gion feels like stepping back in time, with its charming atmosphere and the occasional sighting of a geisha or maiko gracefully making their way to an appointment. It's a reminder of Kyoto's unique blend of past and present.

Finally, end your day with a visit to Fushimi Inari Taisha, renowned for its thousands of vibrant red torii gates that create a mesmerizing pathway up the sacred Mount Inari. As you ascend through the gates, you'll feel a sense of awe and reverence, surrounded by the whispers of history and spirituality. It's a fitting conclusion to your exploration of Kyoto, leaving you with a deeper understanding and appreciation of Japan's rich cultural tapestry.

In Kyoto, every corner offers a new discovery, a new story waiting to be told. Whether you're captivated by the serenity of its temples, the beauty of its crafts, or the quiet elegance of its tea houses, Kyoto promises an unforgettable experience that will linger in your heart long after you've left.

● OSAKA: FOOD HEAVEN AND VIBRANT NIGHTLIFE

As the sun sets over the bustling city of Osaka, the streets come alive with a symphony of sizzling sounds and tantalizing aromas. Known as Japan's culinary capital, Osaka is a food lover's paradise, where every corner offers a new taste sensation waiting to be discovered. From the iconic street food stalls of Dotonbori to the hidden izakayas in the back alleys, this city invites you to indulge in its rich and diverse flavors.

Begin your culinary adventure with a stroll down Dotonbori, a vibrant district that epitomizes Osaka's love for food. Here, the neon lights reflect off the canal, creating a dazzling display that sets the stage for a gastronomic journey. The air is thick with the scent of takoyaki, delicious octopus-filled balls that are a must-try. As you navigate the lively streets, let the calls of vendors entice you to sample okonomiyaki, a savory pancake filled with your choice of ingredients, from succulent pork to fresh seafood. These dishes are not just meals; they're an experience, a taste of Osaka's heart and soul.

But Osaka's culinary delights don't end with street food. Venture into the city's many izakayas, informal Japanese pubs, where locals gather after work to unwind. Here, you can savor a variety of small dishes, from grilled skewers of chicken known as yakitori to the delicate flavors of sashimi. The atmosphere is warm and welcoming, often filled with laughter and the clinking of glasses. Don't be shy—join in the camaraderie and perhaps make a new friend or two. The locals are often eager to share their favorite spots and dishes, offering you an insider's view of Osaka's vibrant food scene.

As the night deepens, Osaka's nightlife beckons with its unique blend of modern and traditional entertainment. Head to Namba, the city's entertainment district, where you can find everything from trendy bars to karaoke joints. If you're looking for a more traditional experience, consider visiting a kabuki theater for a captivating performance that showcases Japan's rich theatrical heritage. The juxtaposition of old and new is a testament to Osaka's dynamic spirit, a city that embraces its history while eagerly looking to the future.

For those seeking a quieter evening, a leisurely walk along the Osaka Castle grounds offers a serene escape. Illuminated at night, the castle stands as a majestic reminder of the city's storied past. As you stroll through the surrounding park, take a moment to reflect on the blend of history and modernity that defines Osaka, a city that never ceases to surprise and delight.

In Osaka, every meal is an invitation to explore, every street a new adventure waiting to be uncovered. Whether you're a seasoned foodie or a curious traveler, this city promises to satisfy your palate and ignite your senses. So, embrace the spirit of kuidaore—to eat oneself into ruin—and let Osaka's culinary wonders guide you through a night you won't soon forget.

• LESSER-KNOWN DESTINATIONS FOR A UNIQUE EXPERIENCE

When venturing beyond the well-trodden paths of Tokyo, Kyoto, and Osaka, Japan reveals a tapestry of hidden gems that promise an experience like no other. These lesser-known destinations offer a glimpse into the heart of Japan, where tradition and nature coexist in harmony, waiting to be explored by the curious traveler.

Imagine stepping into the serene landscapes of Tottori, a prefecture often overlooked by tourists. Here, the majestic Tottori Sand Dunes stretch across the coast, offering a surreal desert-like experience. As you walk along the dunes, the sea breeze on your face, you might feel as though you've been transported to another world. Don't miss the opportunity to try sandboarding or take a camel ride, adding a dash of adventure to your visit.

Further west, the quaint town of Matsue in Shimane Prefecture beckons with its rich history and tranquil beauty. Known as the "City of Water," Matsue is surrounded by lakes and canals, perfect for a leisurely boat ride. Visit the Matsue Castle, one of Japan's few remaining original castles, and stroll through the picturesque streets lined with traditional samurai houses. The town's charm is amplified by the warm hospitality of its residents, making it an ideal place to experience authentic Japanese culture.

For those seeking a spiritual journey, the sacred island of Shikoku offers the famous 88 Temple Pilgrimage. This ancient route winds through lush mountains and serene villages, providing a profound sense of peace and reflection. While completing the entire pilgrimage is a formidable task, even visiting a few temples allows you to connect with Japan's spiritual heritage. The journey is as much about the people you meet and the stories you share as it is about the destination itself.

In the north, the untouched beauty of Hokkaido awaits. Known for its stunning natural landscapes, Hokkaido is a paradise for outdoor enthusiasts. During the winter months, the region transforms into a snowy wonderland, perfect for skiing and snowboarding. In the summer, the rolling fields of lavender in Furano and the crystal-clear waters of Lake Toya offer breathtaking vistas. Hokkaido's unique blend of rugged wilderness and serene beauty is a testament to Japan's diverse landscapes.

Heading south, the island of Kyushu offers a different flavor of Japan. The city of Nagasaki, with its poignant history and vibrant multicultural influences, provides a unique perspective on Japan's past and present. Meanwhile, the volcanic landscapes of Mount Aso and the lush greenery of Yakushima Island, a UNESCO World Heritage site, showcase the island's natural wonders. Kyushu's culinary delights, from hearty ramen to fresh seafood, are sure to tantalize your taste buds and leave you craving more.

In the heart of Japan lies the lesser-known Gifu Prefecture, home to the enchanting village of Shirakawa-go. Nestled in the mountains, this UNESCO World Heritage site is famous for its traditional gassho-zukuri farmhouses, with steep thatched roofs designed to withstand heavy snowfall. Visiting Shirakawa-go in winter, when the village is blanketed in snow and illuminated by warm lights, feels like stepping into a fairytale.

As you explore these hidden corners of Japan, remember that the journey is just as important as the destination. Take the time to engage with the locals, savor regional delicacies, and immerse yourself in the unique customs and traditions that make each place special. Whether it's sharing a cup of tea with a friendly shopkeeper or participating in a local festival, these moments of connection will enrich your travel experience and leave you with memories to cherish.

In a country as diverse and captivating as Japan, the lesser-known destinations offer a chance to step off the beaten path and discover the true essence of Japan. Embrace the unknown, and let the spirit of adventure guide you to places where the stories of Japan's past and present come alive in the most unexpected ways.

Outdoor Adventures: Exploring Japan's Natural Wonders

Imagine standing amidst the towering peaks of the Japanese Alps, the crisp mountain air filling your lungs, and the sounds of nature enveloping you. Japan's natural beauty is a tapestry of majestic landscapes and serene vistas, waiting to be explored. From the lush forests of Yakushima to the volcanic wonders of Hokkaido, outdoor adventures abound.

One of the most exhilarating experiences is hiking the Kumano Kodo, an ancient pilgrimage route in the Kii Mountain Range. As you trek through sacred forests and past centuries-old shrines, you'll feel a deep connection to Japan's spiritual heritage. The trails, though challenging, offer a profound sense of tranquility and reflection.

For those who prefer the sea, the coastal beauty of Okinawa beckons. Here, the azure waters and vibrant coral reefs invite you to dive into an underwater paradise. Snorkeling and diving reveal a world teeming with marine life, where time seems to slow down, allowing you to savor the moment.

Whether you're scaling mountains or exploring coastal wonders, Japan's natural landscapes promise an adventure that's as enriching as it is unforgettable. Embrace the journey, and let the land of the rising sun unveil its hidden treasures.

● ICONIC HIKES AND NATURE WALKS

Imagine standing at the base of Mt. Fuji, Japan's most iconic peak, as the first light of dawn begins to paint the sky in hues of pink and gold. This is not just a hike; it's a journey into the heart of Japan's spirit. Whether you're an experienced climber or a casual walker, the ascent of Mt. Fuji offers a unique blend of challenge and serenity. The official climbing season runs from July to September, where the trails are open and the weather is most favorable. As you climb, the landscape shifts from lush greenery to rocky terrain, culminating in a view from the summit that is nothing short of breathtaking. Remember to start your ascent early in the morning to catch the sunrise from the top—a moment that many describe as a spiritual awakening.

For those seeking a more tranquil experience, the Nakasendo Trail offers a historical journey through Japan's countryside. Once a vital link between Kyoto and Edo (modern-day Tokyo), this ancient route takes you through picturesque villages, lush forests, and past the serene Kiso Valley. Walking the Nakasendo is like stepping back in time; you'll pass by traditional wooden inns, known as ryokan, where weary travelers once rested. Each step along this trail is an opportunity to connect with Japan's rich history and enjoy the natural beauty that has remained unchanged for centuries. Be sure to stop in the charming post towns of Magome and Tsumago, where you can experience the hospitality and warmth of local culture.

Japan's natural beauty extends beyond its famous mountains and trails. The Kamikochi Valley in the Northern Japan Alps is a haven for nature lovers. Known for its stunning vistas, the valley is crisscrossed by clear rivers and surrounded by majestic peaks. The hiking trails here vary in difficulty, making it accessible for all levels of hikers. As you wander through the valley, keep an eye out for the diverse wildlife, including the playful Japanese macaques and the elusive serow. The tranquil atmosphere of Kamikochi is perfect for those who wish to escape the hustle and bustle of city life and immerse themselves in nature's embrace.

For a truly off-the-beaten-path adventure, consider exploring the Kumano Kodo, a network of ancient pilgrimage routes that weave through the Kii Peninsula. These trails, which have been walked by pilgrims for over a thousand years, are now a UNESCO World

Heritage site. The Kumano Kodo offers a deeply spiritual experience, with paths that lead to sacred shrines nestled within the forested hills. As you walk, you'll encounter moss-covered stone steps, towering cedar trees, and the soothing sounds of nature. The journey is as much about the inner reflection as it is about the physical challenge, making it a profoundly moving experience.

Each of these hikes and nature walks offers a distinct perspective on Japan's diverse landscapes and cultural heritage. Whether you're drawn to the challenge of climbing Mt. Fuji, the historical allure of the Nakasendo Trail, the serene beauty of Kamikochi, or the spiritual journey of the Kumano Kodo, you'll find that these experiences are more than just walks in nature—they are pathways to understanding Japan's soul. As you lace up your hiking boots and set out on these trails, remember to embrace the journey, savor each moment, and let the natural beauty of Japan inspire and rejuvenate your spirit.

• NATIONAL PARKS AND HOT SPRINGS (ONSEN): WHAT TO EXPECT

As you step into the serene realms of Japan's national parks and hot springs (onsen), you're entering a world where nature and tradition blend seamlessly. These sanctuaries offer a retreat into the heart of Japan's natural beauty, steeped in cultural significance and healing properties. Whether you're a seasoned traveler or a curious first-timer, knowing what to expect can transform your visit into an unforgettable experience.

Japan's national parks are a testament to the country's diverse landscapes. From the volcanic peaks of Hokkaido to the lush forests of Kyushu, each park offers a unique glimpse into the country's natural wonders. Imagine hiking through the ancient cedar forests of Yakushima, where towering trees and misty air create an otherworldly atmosphere. Or picture yourself standing on the edge of Lake Ashi in Hakone, with the iconic Mount Fuji as your backdrop. These parks are not just about breathtaking vistas; they are a gateway to understanding Japan's deep respect for nature.

When visiting these parks, it's essential to embrace the Japanese concept of 'Shinrin-yoku', or forest bathing. This practice encourages you to immerse yourself fully in the natural environment, absorbing the sights, sounds, and scents of the forest. It's a meditative experience, one that refreshes the mind and spirit, and it's something that Japan's national parks offer in abundance. Whether you're taking a leisurely stroll or embarking on a challenging hike, allow yourself to slow down and connect with the natural world around you.

After a day of exploring, there's no better way to unwind than by soaking in an onsen. These hot springs are a quintessential part of Japanese culture, offering both relaxation and a sense of communal harmony. As you slip into the warm, mineral-rich waters, you'll feel the stresses of the day melt away. Onsens are often located in picturesque settings, surrounded by mountains, rivers, or coastal views, adding to the tranquility of the experience.

While the prospect of communal bathing might seem daunting to some, it's an opportunity to embrace a cultural tradition that dates back centuries. Onsens are places of quiet reflection and social connection, where the boundaries of everyday life dissolve. It's important to follow the etiquette: rinse off before entering the bath, keep your towel out of the water, and maintain a respectful silence. These customs ensure that everyone can enjoy the onsen's soothing properties.

For those seeking a more private experience, many ryokans (traditional Japanese inns) offer rooms with their own private onsen baths. This allows you to enjoy the therapeutic benefits of the hot springs in solitude, with the added luxury of staying in a beautifully designed room that often features tatami mats and shoji screens. Whether you choose a communal or private onsen, the key is to relax and let the natural warmth rejuvenate your body and soul.

Exploring Japan's national parks and onsens is not just about the physical journey; it's about immersing yourself in a way of life that values harmony with nature. These experiences provide a deeper understanding of Japan's cultural heritage and offer a respite from the hustle and bustle of modern life. As you plan your visit, remember to pack light, wear comfortable clothing, and bring an open mind. The landscapes and traditions you encounter will leave a lasting impression, inviting you to return to the heart of the Rising Sun time and again.

• BEST BEACHES AND COASTAL RETREATS

As you journey through Japan, the allure of its vibrant cities and historic landmarks might capture your attention, but the country's coastal retreats offer an equally captivating escape. Japan's beaches are a blend of natural beauty, cultural richness, and tranquility, providing a refreshing contrast to urban life. Whether you're seeking relaxation, adventure, or a touch of both, Japan's coastlines promise an unforgettable experience.

One of the most stunning coastal destinations is Okinawa, an archipelago renowned for its crystal-clear waters and white sandy beaches. Okinawa's unique charm lies in its subtropical climate, which offers a year-round paradise for beach lovers. Here, you can indulge in snorkeling or diving in the vibrant coral reefs, home to a dazzling array of marine life. The island's laid-back atmosphere and rich Ryukyu culture add a layer of depth to your visit, inviting you to explore its history and savor its distinctive cuisine.

Moving north, the Shonan Coast near Tokyo is a favorite among locals and tourists alike. With its relaxed vibe and stunning views of Mount Fuji, Shonan offers a perfect getaway from the bustling city. Enoshima Island, connected to the mainland by a bridge, is a highlight of the area. Its scenic lighthouse and botanical gardens provide a peaceful retreat, while the island's traditional shrines offer a glimpse into Japan's spiritual heritage. As you stroll along the beach, the gentle waves and refreshing sea breeze create an idyllic setting for reflection and rejuvenation.

For those seeking a more secluded experience, the Noto Peninsula in Ishikawa Prefecture is a hidden gem waiting to be discovered. The rugged coastline, with its dramatic cliffs and serene beaches, offers a sense of adventure and solitude. Noto's unspoiled landscapes are perfect for hiking and exploring, while the region's rich cultural traditions, such as the Wajima lacquerware and the Kiriko festivals, provide a deeper connection to the local way of life.

On the western coast, Shirahama in Wakayama Prefecture is famed for its hot springs and beautiful beaches. The name "Shirahama" translates to "white beach," and its pristine sands live up to the name. The area is also home to Adventure World, a family-friendly attraction featuring a zoo and aquarium. After a day of exploration, relax in one of the many onsen (hot springs) that the region is known for, letting the mineral-rich waters soothe your body and mind.

Japan's northernmost island, Hokkaido, offers a different kind of coastal charm. While it may not be the first place that comes to mind for beachgoers, Hokkaido's rugged shores and cool climate provide a unique experience. The Shiretoko Peninsula, a UNESCO World Heritage site, boasts breathtaking coastal scenery and abundant wildlife. Here, you can embark on a guided boat tour to spot seals, sea eagles, and even the occasional bear along the shoreline. The untouched natural beauty of Hokkaido's coasts is a testament to the island's wild and pristine environment.

Each of these coastal retreats offers a distinct flavor of Japan's diverse landscapes. Whether you're basking in the sun on Okinawa's beaches, exploring the cultural richness of the Noto Peninsula, or marveling at the natural wonders of Hokkaido, Japan's coastlines promise a journey filled with discovery and relaxation. As you plan your visit, remember to embrace the local customs and savor the unique experiences that each destination has to offer. From the soothing rhythm of the waves to the captivating stories of the people you meet, Japan's beaches are more than just a scenic escape—they are a gateway to the heart and soul of the country.

● TIPS FOR SUSTAINABLE AND ECO-FRIENDLY TRAVEL

As you prepare for your journey across Japan, it's essential to consider the impact of your travels on the environment. Embracing sustainable and eco-friendly travel practices not only helps preserve the beauty of Japan for future generations but also enriches your travel experience. By making conscious choices, you can connect more deeply with the places you visit and the people you meet.

One of the simplest ways to travel sustainably in Japan is by using its extensive public transportation network. The country's trains and buses are not only efficient and reliable but also a more eco-friendly option compared to renting a car. The Japan Rail Pass is an excellent investment for those planning to explore multiple cities. It offers unlimited travel on most trains, including the famed

Shinkansen or bullet trains, which are both a marvel of engineering and a symbol of sustainable travel with their reduced carbon footprint.

If you're exploring cities like Tokyo or Kyoto, consider renting a bicycle. Many Japanese cities are becoming increasingly bike-friendly, with dedicated lanes and rental services available at reasonable prices. Cycling not only reduces your carbon emissions but also allows you to experience the city at a more leisurely pace, discovering hidden gems tucked away in quiet neighborhoods.

When it comes to accommodations, look for hotels and inns that are committed to sustainability. Many traditional ryokans and modern hotels in Japan have adopted eco-friendly practices, such as using solar energy, reducing water usage, and supporting local agriculture. Staying at these places not only supports their efforts but also provides you with a more authentic experience, often accompanied by locally sourced meals that reflect the region's culinary heritage.

Speaking of meals, Japan offers a fantastic opportunity to enjoy seasonal and locally sourced food. By choosing dishes made with ingredients that are in season, you not only enjoy fresher and more flavorful meals but also support local farmers and reduce the carbon footprint associated with importing goods. Visit local markets, such as the famous Tsukiji Outer Market in Tokyo or Nishiki Market in Kyoto, to sample fresh produce and regional specialties.

Another way to travel sustainably is by reducing waste. Japan is known for its meticulous waste separation and recycling practices, and you can contribute by carrying a reusable water bottle and shopping bag. Many public places have water fountains, and convenience stores often offer refills, making it easy to stay hydrated without purchasing plastic bottles. Similarly, a reusable shopping bag can help you avoid unnecessary plastic when shopping for souvenirs or snacks.

Engaging with the local culture and community is also a vital component of sustainable travel. Consider participating in community-based tourism activities, such as volunteering for local projects or joining workshops that teach traditional crafts. These experiences not only support local economies but also provide you with a deeper understanding of Japan's rich cultural heritage.

Lastly, be mindful of your impact on natural sites. Japan is home to breathtaking landscapes, from the iconic Mount Fuji to the serene beaches of Okinawa. While visiting these places, stick to marked paths to avoid damaging the environment, and follow the principles of Leave No Trace. By respecting nature and minimizing your footprint, you help preserve these sites for others to enjoy.

Traveling sustainably in Japan is about making thoughtful choices that enhance your journey while respecting the environment and culture. By incorporating these practices into your trip, you'll not only have a more fulfilling experience but also contribute to the preservation of Japan's natural and cultural treasures for generations to come. Remember, every small step counts, and your efforts can inspire others to follow suit.

CULTURAL IMMERSION: TRADITIONS AND EXPERIENCES

Picture yourself stepping into a serene tea house in Kyoto, where the gentle rustle of kimono fabric and the delicate aroma of matcha envelop you. This is not just a tea ceremony; it's an immersive experience into the heart of Japanese tradition. Here, every gesture is a dance, every sip a meditation, inviting you to slow down and appreciate the artistry of the moment. As you observe the tea master, you learn that this ritual is about more than just tea—it's a reflection of Japanese philosophy, emphasizing harmony and respect.

Venture further into the countryside, where the ancient art of calligraphy awaits. Under the guidance of a skilled sensei, you'll discover that each stroke of the brush is a journey of self-expression. The quiet concentration required in this practice mirrors Japan's cultural emphasis on mindfulness and patience. As you create your first kanji, you'll feel a connection to the centuries of tradition that have shaped this art.

And then, there's the vibrant festival atmosphere. Imagine the streets of Osaka during a lively matsuri, where the air is filled with the sounds of taiko drums and the tantalizing scent of street food. Joining the locals in celebration, you'll experience the communal joy and energy that define these festivals, offering a glimpse into the collective spirit of Japan.

• PARTICIPATING IN LOCAL FESTIVALS AND EVENTS

Imagine yourself standing amidst a sea of vibrant colors, the air filled with the rhythmic beat of drums and the cheerful laughter of people from all walks of life. Participating in local festivals and events in Japan is not just about witnessing a spectacle; it's about becoming part of a living tapestry of culture and tradition that has been woven over centuries. These festivals, known as matsuri, offer a unique glimpse into the heart of Japanese society, where ancient customs meet modern-day celebrations.

(On page 233 you will find a list with more than 25 national and local events and festivals for each time of year)

One of the most enchanting aspects of Japanese festivals is their ability to transform everyday spaces into realms of magic and wonder. Streets become stages for dynamic parades, with participants dressed in elaborate costumes, often representing historical or mythical figures. The energy is palpable, and as a visitor, you are encouraged to join in the festivities, whether it's by clapping along to the music or even participating in a traditional dance.

Take the Gion Matsuri in Kyoto, for example. Held annually in July, this festival is a grand celebration that dates back over a thousand years. The highlight is the Yamaboko Junko, a procession of towering floats intricately decorated and pulled through the streets by teams of locals. As you stand among the crowd, you'll feel the deep sense of community and pride that permeates the air, a testament to the dedication and craftsmanship involved in preparing for this event.

For a more intimate experience, consider attending a smaller, local festival. These often focus on specific traditions, such as the Obon festival, which honors the spirits of ancestors. Held in August, Obon is marked by the Bon Odori dance, where people gather in a circle to perform simple, graceful movements. Participating in this dance is a beautiful way to connect with the local community and experience the spiritual side of Japanese culture.

Food is another integral part of any festival, and Japanese matsuri are no exception. Stalls line the festival grounds, offering an array of delicious treats that are as much a feast for the eyes as they are for the palate. From takoyaki (octopus balls) to yakisoba (fried noodles), these culinary delights provide a taste of Japan's rich gastronomic heritage. Don't be shy to try something new—each bite is a step deeper into the cultural experience.

While language barriers might seem daunting, Japanese festivals are incredibly welcoming to visitors. Many locals are eager to share their traditions and may even offer to teach you a few phrases or gestures to help you join in the fun. Remember, the key to enjoying these events is to approach them with an open heart and a willingness to learn.

It's also important to be mindful of local customs and etiquette. For instance, when attending a festival, it's customary to dress modestly and comfortably, often in a yukata, a casual summer kimono. You might find rental shops near major festivals where you can don this traditional attire, adding to the authenticity of your experience.

Participating in a Japanese festival is not just an activity; it's an invitation to step into a world where history, culture, and community come alive in the most vibrant way possible. As you wander through the lively streets, surrounded by the joyous sounds and sights, you'll find yourself not just observing but becoming part of a story that has been told for generations. It is in these moments that the true essence of Japan reveals itself, leaving you with memories that will linger long after the festival lights have dimmed.

● Visiting temples, shrines, and UNESCO World Heritage sites

Stepping into a Japanese temple or shrine is like walking into a living tapestry of history and spirituality. Each site tells its own story, whispering tales of ancient rituals and revered deities. The air is often filled with the gentle sound of wind chimes, and the scent of incense lingers, creating a serene atmosphere that invites reflection and peace.

When you visit these sacred places, you'll often start at the torii gate, a symbolic entrance that marks the transition from the mundane to the sacred. As you pass through, remember to pause and bow slightly, acknowledging the sanctity of the space you are entering. This simple gesture is a mark of respect and a way to connect with the spiritual essence of the site.

One of the most iconic experiences is visiting the Kinkaku-ji, or the Golden Pavilion, in Kyoto. The way the sunlight glints off its gold leaf exterior is nothing short of breathtaking. As you stroll around the mirror-like pond, take a moment to appreciate how nature and architecture harmoniously blend here, reflecting the Japanese aesthetic of wabi-sabi, the beauty of imperfection.

In Nara, the Todai-ji Temple houses the Great Buddha, a colossal statue that radiates tranquility. As you stand before this awe-inspiring figure, let yourself be enveloped by the sense of calm and reverence that fills the hall. It's a humbling reminder of the enduring power of faith and craftsmanship.

Japan's shrines, such as the famous Fushimi Inari-taisha in Kyoto, offer a different but equally captivating experience. Known for its thousands of red torii gates, this shrine is dedicated to Inari, the deity of rice and prosperity. Walking through the winding paths of the gates, you'll feel as though you are being led into a mystical realm. Each gate is donated by individuals or businesses, a testament to the continuing relevance of these spiritual sites in modern life.

When visiting these places, it's important to observe a few customs. At the entrance of many temples and shrines, you'll find a temizuya, a water pavilion where you can purify yourself before entering. Use the ladle to pour water over your hands and rinse your mouth, a ritual that cleanses both body and spirit.

Inside the temple or shrine, you may wish to offer a prayer or make a small donation. At a shrine, toss a coin into the offering box, bow twice, clap twice, and then bow once more after your prayer. This rhythmic sequence is a respectful way to communicate with the deities. In temples, a quiet moment of reflection or meditation is appropriate, allowing you to absorb the peaceful energy of the surroundings.

For those interested in Japan's UNESCO World Heritage sites, the Historic Monuments of Ancient Kyoto and the Himeji Castle are must-sees. Himeji Castle, with its elegant white facade and intricate architecture, is a marvel of feudal Japan. As you explore its corridors and climb its towers, imagine the samurai who once walked these paths, defending the castle and their honor.

While these grand sites are awe-inspiring, don't overlook the smaller, less frequented temples and shrines scattered throughout the country. These hidden gems often offer a more intimate experience, allowing you to connect with the local community and the quieter side of Japanese spirituality.

As you journey through these sacred spaces, remember that you are not just a visitor but a participant in a living tradition. By showing respect and openness, you'll find that these temples and shrines offer not just a glimpse into Japan's past but also a deeper understanding of its cultural soul.

• UNDERSTANDING TEA CEREMONIES AND OTHER CULTURAL RITUALS

Imagine stepping into a serene room, where the air is filled with the delicate aroma of freshly brewed tea and the gentle rustle of silk. This is the world of the Japanese tea ceremony, or chanoyu, a ritual that is as much about the heart as it is about the tea itself. The tea ceremony is a cornerstone of Japanese culture, embodying the principles of harmony, respect, purity, and tranquility. It is an art form that has been meticulously refined over centuries, offering a window into the soul of Japan.

As you prepare to experience a tea ceremony, it's important to understand that it is not merely about drinking tea. It is a deeply symbolic practice that reflects the Japanese appreciation for simplicity and mindfulness. Every movement is deliberate, every gesture meaningful, as the host and guests engage in a silent dialogue of respect and understanding.

Upon entering the tea room, or chashitsu, you are greeted by an atmosphere of calm and simplicity. The room is typically small, with tatami mats covering the floor and minimal decoration. A scroll hangs in the alcove, known as the tokonoma, often bearing a Zen phrase or seasonal artwork, setting the tone for the gathering. Fresh flowers, arranged simply, add a touch of nature, reminding participants of the beauty in transience.

The ceremony begins with the host preparing the tea utensils, each item carefully chosen and placed with precision. The tea bowl, whisk, scoop, and caddy are not just tools but objects of art, often crafted by skilled artisans. The host's movements are slow and deliberate, a dance of grace and attentiveness that invites the guests to enter a state of meditation.

As a guest, you are an integral part of this ritual. Your role is to engage with the ceremony respectfully, observing the host's actions and responding with gratitude. When the tea is served, you take the bowl with both hands, turning it slightly before taking a sip. This gesture of turning the bowl demonstrates humility and appreciation for the effort that has gone into the preparation of the tea.

The flavor of the tea, typically a powdered green tea known as matcha, is rich and earthy, offering a moment of reflection as you savor its taste. Conversation is minimal, often limited to expressions of gratitude and admiration for the host's skill. This silence is not awkward but rather a shared understanding of the ceremony's deeper significance.

Beyond the tea ceremony, Japan is home to a myriad of other cultural rituals that offer similar insights into its values and traditions. From the rhythmic art of taiko drumming to the graceful movements of noh theater, each ritual is a testament to Japan's rich cultural tapestry. These experiences invite you to step out of the rush of modern life and into a space where time seems to stand still, allowing you to connect with the essence of Japanese culture.

Participating in these rituals may seem daunting, especially if you are unfamiliar with the customs. However, remember that the Japanese are incredibly welcoming and appreciative of those who show genuine interest and respect for their traditions. Do not worry about making mistakes; instead, approach each experience with an open heart and a willingness to learn.

Understanding and participating in Japan's cultural rituals offers a unique opportunity to see the world from a different perspective. It allows you to experience firsthand the values that have shaped Japanese society for centuries. Whether you are sipping tea in a tranquil garden or watching a noh performance under the night sky, these moments will leave you with a deeper appreciation for the beauty of Japan's traditions.

As you continue your journey through Japan, let these experiences guide you, opening your eyes to the subtleties of Japanese culture and the profound lessons they hold. Embrace the opportunity to learn and grow, and you will find that the heart of the Rising Sun is not just a destination, but a journey of discovery and connection.

• ENGAGING WITH LOCAL ARTISANS AND CRAFTSPEOPLE

As you wander through the bustling streets of Japan, from the vibrant alleys of Tokyo to the serene paths of Kyoto, you will find yourself inevitably drawn to the intricate world of local artisans and craftspeople. These skilled individuals are the custodians of Japan's rich cultural heritage, crafting items that tell stories of tradition, innovation, and dedication. Engaging with these artisans is not just about purchasing a souvenir; it's about connecting with the very soul of Japan.

Imagine stepping into a traditional pottery studio in the heart of Kyoto. The air is filled with the earthy scent of clay, and you're greeted by the warm smile of a potter whose hands have shaped thousands of pieces over the decades. Here, you can witness the delicate dance of the potter's wheel as it spins clay into graceful forms. The potter may invite you to try your hand at crafting your own piece, guiding you with gentle patience. It's a rare opportunity to not only learn a new skill but to gain insight into the meticulous work that goes into each item.

In the vibrant city of Osaka, you might find yourself in a textile workshop, surrounded by bolts of colorful fabric. The artisans here are masters of weaving, dyeing, and embroidery, using techniques passed down through generations. They might demonstrate the art of indigo dyeing, a traditional practice that transforms plain fabric into a deep, rich blue. As you watch, you'll gain a deeper appreciation for the patience and precision required to create these beautiful textiles.

Tokyo, with its blend of modernity and tradition, offers a unique chance to explore the world of contemporary artisans. In a small studio tucked away in a quiet neighborhood, you might meet a young craftsman who combines traditional techniques with modern design to create stunning pieces of jewelry or home decor. These artisans are not only preserving age-old techniques but also pushing the boundaries, ensuring that Japanese craftsmanship remains relevant and vibrant in today's world.

Venturing into the countryside, you may stumble upon a woodworking shop where the scent of cedar and pine lingers in the air. Here, artisans shape wood into everything from delicate chopsticks to intricate furniture. You'll see how each piece of wood is carefully selected and worked on, respecting its natural grain and character. Engaging with these craftspeople provides a glimpse into the sustainable practices that have been at the heart of Japanese craftsmanship for centuries.

Beyond the workshops and studios, engaging with local artisans also means participating in seasonal markets and festivals. These vibrant gatherings are a feast for the senses, where artisans proudly display their creations. It's a chance to speak directly with the makers, learn about their inspirations, and perhaps even witness a live demonstration of their craft. Such experiences are not only enriching but also foster a deeper connection to the local community.

As you explore these artisanal worlds, remember that your interactions are a two-way street. Show respect and genuine interest in their work, and you'll often find that artisans are eager to share their knowledge and stories with you. This cultural exchange enriches your journey, offering insights into the values and traditions that shape Japan.

Engaging with local artisans and craftspeople is a rewarding experience that goes beyond mere observation. It is an invitation to participate in a living tradition, to understand the dedication and passion that go into each handcrafted piece. Whether you leave with a handmade bowl, a beautifully dyed scarf, or simply cherished memories, you carry with you a piece of Japan's cultural heritage, a testament to the artisans who continue to breathe life into their crafts.

SHOPPING IN JAPAN: FROM SOUVENIRS TO LUXURY GOODS

Stepping into the vibrant world of Japanese shopping is like embarking on a treasure hunt where every corner offers something unique and unexpected. From bustling street markets to the serene elegance of traditional craft shops, Japan is a shopper's paradise. Imagine wandering through the lively streets of Tokyo's Harajuku, where fashion-forward boutiques sit beside quirky vintage stores, each offering a glimpse into the eclectic style that defines this energetic city.

For those seeking a more luxurious experience, the upscale districts of Ginza in Tokyo and Shinsaibashi in Osaka present a dazzling array of high-end brands. Here, the gleaming storefronts of iconic fashion houses beckon with their latest collections, offering a taste of global luxury with a distinctly Japanese twist. Yet, amidst the glamour, you'll find hidden gems—boutiques showcasing local designers whose creations blend traditional techniques with modern aesthetics.

No shopping journey in Japan is complete without indulging in the art of souvenir hunting. Whether it's a finely crafted ceramic tea set from Kyoto or a beautifully packaged box of matcha sweets, these treasures carry the essence of Japan. Each item tells a story, a tangible memory of your journey through the Land of the Rising Sun.

• ICONIC JAPANESE PRODUCTS: ELECTRONICS, FASHION, AND TRADITIONAL ITEMS

Exploring the heart of Japan often leads travelers to the allure of its iconic products. From cutting-edge electronics to exquisite fashion and timeless traditional items, Japan offers a diverse array of goods that reflect its rich cultural tapestry and innovative spirit.

When it comes to electronics, Japan stands as a global powerhouse. Cities like Tokyo and Osaka are dotted with bustling electronic districts where you can find everything from the latest gadgets to rare tech treasures. Akihabara, often dubbed the mecca of electronics, is a labyrinth of neon-lit shops offering everything from high-end cameras to quirky electronic toys. Whether you're a tech enthusiast or a casual shopper, the thrill of discovering a unique gadget in these bustling markets is an experience in itself.

Japan's influence in the world of fashion is equally profound. The streets of Harajuku in Tokyo are a kaleidoscope of color and creativity, where avant-garde fashion meets traditional attire. Here, you'll witness an eclectic mix of styles, from the bold and experimental to the elegantly classic. Japanese fashion brands have earned a reputation for their impeccable craftsmanship and innovative designs. Whether it's the minimalist elegance of Uniqlo or the high-fashion allure of Comme des Garçons, there's something to suit every taste and style.

The charm of Japan extends beyond the modern to its traditional items, which hold a special place in the hearts of both locals and travelers. The art of crafting has been passed down through generations, resulting in exquisite products that embody the essence of Japanese culture. Consider the delicate beauty of a hand-painted kimono or the intricate design of a handcrafted tea set. Such items are not merely souvenirs; they are pieces of history and art that offer a glimpse into Japan's rich heritage.

For those seeking a deeper connection with Japanese culture, exploring the world of traditional crafts is a must. Visit Kyoto's Nishijin district to witness the creation of beautiful textiles or explore the pottery studios in the countryside where artisans shape clay into stunning ceramics. These experiences provide not only an opportunity to purchase unique items but also a chance to appreciate the skill and dedication that go into each piece.

As you journey through Japan, remember that each product you encounter is a reflection of the country's unique blend of tradition and innovation. Whether you're navigating the bustling streets of Tokyo or exploring the serene landscapes of Kyoto, the treasures you discover will offer you a deeper understanding of Japan's vibrant culture and enduring legacy. Embrace the opportunity to bring a piece of Japan home with you, a reminder of your unforgettable journey into the heart of Japan.

• BEST SHOPPING DISTRICTS IN TOKYO, OSAKA AND KYOTO

When it comes to shopping in Japan, each city offers its own unique flavor and charm. Tokyo, with its sprawling metropolis, is a shopper's paradise where tradition meets modernity. Begin your journey in Shibuya, where the iconic crossing sets the stage for a vibrant shopping experience. Here, you can explore the latest fashion trends at Shibuya 109, a towering fashion hub that caters to the youth and the young at heart. Just a stone's throw away, Harajuku awaits with its eclectic mix of quirky boutiques and vintage stores along Takeshita Street. For those seeking luxury, Ginza offers high-end brands and flagship stores housed in sleek, sophisticated buildings.

In contrast, Osaka presents a more laid-back yet equally enticing shopping scene. The bustling Shinsaibashi district is a must-visit, where you can wander through endless arcades filled with everything from trendy apparel to unique souvenirs. Don't miss the chance to visit Amerikamura, or "Amemura," known for its bohemian vibe and a plethora of vintage shops and cafes that exude a youthful energy. If you're a fan of electronics and gadgets, a stroll through Nipponbashi, Osaka's answer to Tokyo's Akihabara, will leave you in awe of the latest technological marvels.

Meanwhile, Kyoto offers a shopping experience that is deeply rooted in tradition. The Nishiki Market is a feast for the senses, where you can indulge in local delicacies and pick up artisanal crafts. As you wander through the market's narrow alleys, you'll find everything from handcrafted knives to delicate ceramics. For a more serene shopping experience, head to Gion, where traditional tea houses and shops selling exquisite kimono and textiles line the streets. Here, you can immerse yourself in the elegance of Kyoto's cultural heritage.

Regardless of where you choose to shop, remember that tax-free shopping is available for tourists in many stores, so be sure to bring your passport. Also, while credit cards are widely accepted in major cities, having some cash on hand is always a good idea, especially when venturing into smaller shops or markets.

Shopping in Japan is not just about purchasing items; it's a cultural experience that offers a glimpse into the heart of each city. Whether you're hunting for the latest fashions, unique souvenirs, or traditional crafts, you'll find that each district has its own story to tell. So, take your time, explore, and let the vibrant energy of Japan's shopping districts guide you to unexpected treasures.

• WHAT TO BUY AND WHAT TO AVOID (AND HOW TO CLAIM TAX-FREE SHOPPING)

Shopping in Japan can be a delightful adventure, a treasure hunt through bustling streets and serene shops, each offering a unique glimpse into the country's vibrant culture. Whether you're strolling through the neon-lit streets of Shibuya or wandering the quiet lanes of Kyoto, you'll find an array of goods that beckon to be taken home. But with so many options, what should you buy and what should you leave behind?

First, let's talk about what to buy. Japan is renowned for its craftsmanship and attention to detail, so consider items that reflect this. Traditional Japanese ceramics, such as delicate tea sets or beautifully glazed bowls, make for exquisite souvenirs. If you're a fan of textiles, don't miss out on a kimono or a stylish yukata. These garments are not only a piece of art but also a piece of history, each stitch telling a story.

For those with a sweet tooth, Japanese confectioneries are a must. From matcha-flavored treats to mochi with red bean filling, these sweets are a taste of Japan you can savor long after your trip. And let's not forget the world of anime and manga. For pop culture enthusiasts, a visit to Akihabara in Tokyo will reveal a plethora of collectibles and memorabilia.

Now, on to what to avoid. While it might be tempting to buy everything that catches your eye, some items are best left on the shelf. For example, imitation goods or knockoff brands, which are not uncommon in tourist-heavy areas, often lack the quality and authenticity you'd hope for. Additionally, while electronics in Japan are top-notch, they may not always be compatible with systems back home, so be sure to check before purchasing.

When it comes to tax-free shopping, Japan offers a fantastic opportunity to save some yen. Many shops provide tax-free services for tourists, which means you can enjoy a 10% discount on your purchases. To take advantage of this, ensure you have your passport with you, as it's required for the transaction. Look for stores displaying the "Tax-Free Shop" sign and remember that the tax-free option is typically available for purchases over a certain amount, often 5,000 yen.

Once you've made your tax-free purchases, keep the receipts and ensure they remain attached to your passport. These will be checked at customs when you leave the country. It's a straightforward process that allows you to enjoy your shopping spree without the added burden of tax.

In conclusion, shopping in Japan is not just about acquiring goods; it's about bringing a piece of the culture back with you. By choosing wisely and taking advantage of tax-free shopping, you can ensure your souvenirs are both meaningful and budget-friendly. Whether you're drawn to traditional crafts, modern gadgets, or delicious treats, Japan offers something for every traveler to cherish.

• NAVIGATING LOCAL MARKETS AND DEPARTMENT STORES

As you step into the vibrant world of Japan's local markets and department stores, you're not just entering a place to shop—you're diving into a cultural tapestry that offers a glimpse into the daily lives and traditions of the Japanese people. Whether you're wandering through a bustling Asakusa market in Tokyo or exploring the elegant floors of a Kyoto department store, each location offers its own unique blend of the traditional and the modern.

Markets are a sensory delight, brimming with the scent of fresh produce and the lively chatter of vendors. Here, you can discover seasonal fruits like yuzu and persimmons, or try local delicacies such as takoyaki and taiyaki. Don't hesitate to engage with the vendors; most are eager to share their knowledge and offer samples. It's a wonderful way to practice a few Japanese phrases and immerse yourself in the local culture. Remember, a simple "arigato" (thank you) goes a long way.

Department stores, on the other hand, are a testament to Japan's love for quality and service. Often located near major train stations, these multi-story shopping paradises offer everything from high-end fashion to traditional crafts. As you ascend the escalators, you'll find a floor dedicated to exquisite Japanese ceramics, another showcasing cutting-edge electronics, and yet another with gourmet food halls known as depachika. These food basements are a culinary adventure in themselves, offering a vast array of bento boxes, sushi, and confectioneries.

When exploring these spaces, take note of the impeccable customer service. Staff members, known for their omotenashi (hospitality), will greet you with a warm smile and a bow. Even if language barriers arise, their eagerness to assist often transcends words. Don't be shy to use gestures or a translation app to communicate; it's all part of the experience.

For a truly authentic experience, look out for local craft fairs and pop-up markets that often appear in public spaces or temple grounds. These markets are treasure troves of handmade goods, from delicate washi paper to intricately designed kimonos. Purchasing directly from artisans supports local communities and provides you with a unique souvenir that carries a story.

As you navigate these vibrant spaces, remember that each purchase, each interaction, is a step deeper into understanding Japan's rich cultural fabric. So, take your time, explore with an open heart, and let the markets and department stores of Japan reveal their stories to you.

PRACTICAL JAPANESE PHRASES AND CULTURAL TIPS

As you step off the plane and into the vibrant world of Japan, the language may seem like an intricate puzzle. But fear not! Mastering a few practical Japanese phrases and understanding some cultural nuances can transform your journey from daunting to delightful. Picture this: you're in a bustling Tokyo market, the air thick with the enticing aroma of street food. A vendor smiles and offers you a sample. With a simple "Arigatou gozaimasu" (Thank you very much), you convey gratitude, instantly bridging any cultural gap.

Imagine navigating Kyoto's serene temples. As you approach, a gentle nod and a respectful "Sumimasen" (Excuse me) can help you move gracefully through crowds. In Osaka, where the locals are known for their warmth, a friendly "Konnichiwa" (Hello) can open doors to new friendships and experiences. These phrases are more than just words; they are keys to unlocking genuine connections.

Understanding cultural tips is equally crucial. For instance, when dining, remember to say "Itadakimasu" before eating—it's a way to express gratitude for the meal. And when visiting someone's home, removing your shoes at the entrance is a sign of respect.

By embracing these simple phrases and cultural insights, you'll find yourself not just visiting Japan, but truly experiencing it. So, let each word be a step closer to the heart of this beautiful country.

● ESSENTIAL WORDS AND PHRASES FOR NAVIGATING DAILY LIFE

When embarking on your journey through Japan, having a few essential words and phrases at your disposal can be a game-changer. Not only will it help you navigate daily life more smoothly, but it will also enrich your interactions with locals, offering a glimpse into the heart of Japanese culture.

First, let's start with a warm greeting. As you step into any shop or restaurant, a cheerful "Konnichiwa" (こんにちは) will be met with smiles. It means "Hello" and is a great way to start any conversation. If you're greeting someone in the morning, use "Ohayou gozaimasu" (おはようございます) for "Good morning." In the evening, switch to "Konbanwa" (こんばんは) for "Good evening."

Politeness is woven into the fabric of Japanese communication. Mastering the word "Arigato gozaimasu" (ありがとうございます) for "Thank you" will serve you well, whether you're thanking a barista for your coffee or a guide for their assistance. For a more casual thank you among friends, simply say "Arigato" (ありがとう).

When you need to apologize or get someone's attention, saying "Sumimasen" (すみません) is invaluable. It can mean "Excuse me,"

"I'm sorry," or even "Thank you for your trouble," depending on the context. It's a versatile phrase that shows your respect for those around you.

Navigating transportation is a breeze with a few key phrases. If you're lost or need directions, approach someone with a polite "Eigo o hanasemasu ka?" (英語を話せますか？), which means "Do you speak English?" This can be particularly helpful in larger cities where English is more commonly understood. If you're looking for the nearest train station, ask, "Eki wa doko desu ka?" (駅はどこですか？).

When dining out, knowing how to order is essential. Begin with "Kore o kudasai" (これをください) to say "This please," while pointing to the menu item you desire. If you have dietary restrictions or preferences, simply say "Niku wa taberaremasen" (肉は食べられません) if you don't eat meat, or "Vegetarian desu" (ベジタリアンです) to indicate you're vegetarian.

Finally, familiarizing yourself with numbers and basic counting can be incredibly useful, especially when shopping. Understanding how to say numbers like "Ichi" (一) for one, "Ni" (二) for two, and "San" (三) for three will help you navigate prices and quantities.

Remember, even if your pronunciation isn't perfect, your efforts to communicate in Japanese will be appreciated and often met with encouragement. Embrace these phrases as tools to enhance your journey, and you'll find that the language becomes a bridge to deeper cultural connections and memorable experiences.

HELLO KONNICHIWA こんにちは	**I'D LIKE...** ..O KUDASAI ...をください
GOOD MORNING OHAYOU GOZAIMAS おはようございます	**WHAT IS THIS?** KORE WA NAN DES KA? これは何ですか
GOODBYE SAYONARA さようなら	**HOW MUCH IS THIS?** IKURA DES KA? いくらですか?
PLEASE KUDASAI ください	**THE BILL/CHECK, PLEASE** OKAIKEI WO ONEGAISHIMAS お勘定をお願いします
THANK YOU ARIGATO GOZAIMAS ありがとうございます	**WHERE IS THE TOILET?** TOIRE WA DO KO DES KA? トイレはどこですか?
SORRY/EXCUSE ME SUMIMASEN すみません	**YOU ACCEPT CREDIT CARDS?** KUREJITO KADO WA TSUKAEMAS KA? クレジットカードは使えますか?
MY NAME IS... WATASHI NO NAME WA... DES 私の名前は...です	**DO YOU SPEAK ENGLISH?** EIGO WA HANASEMAS KA? 英語を話せますか?
YES HAI はい	**NO** KEKKO DES けっこうです

● UNDERSTANDING CULTURAL NUANCES: BOWING, GIFT-GIVING, AND BODY LANGUAGE

When you step onto the vibrant and bustling streets of Japan, you'll quickly notice that communication extends far beyond just spoken words. The subtle art of cultural nuances, such as bowing, gift-giving, and body language, plays a pivotal role in everyday interactions, shaping the way local people engage with one another and with visitors. Understanding and respecting these customs not only enhances your personal experience but also demonstrates your appreciation for the rich and intricate tapestry of local culture. In a society where tradition and etiquette are highly valued, being mindful of these nuances can lead to more genuine and meaningful exchanges, helping you forge connections that transcend language barriers.

Bowing

Bowing in Japan is more than just a simple greeting; it is a deeply ingrained and multifaceted part of the culture that signifies respect, gratitude, and even apology. The depth, angle, and duration of a bow can vary significantly depending on the context and the relationship between the individuals involved. For instance, a slight nod or a brief bow is common for casual encounters or when meeting acquaintances, while a deeper, longer bow is reserved for formal occasions or when expressing deep respect to someone of higher status. When you find yourself in doubt about how to bow appropriately, a simple, polite bow will usually suffice, as sincerity is often appreciated. It's also a good idea to observe the locals around you and mirror their gestures to ensure you are bowing in a way that aligns with the local customs, helping you navigate social interactions with grace and elegance.

Gift-Giving

Gift-giving in Japan is a cherished tradition that goes well beyond the mere act of exchanging items; it is often used to convey appreciation, strengthen relationships, or mark significant occasions. When presenting a gift, it's customary to offer it with both hands, accompanied by a slight bow, conveying sincerity and respect for the recipient. The presentation of the gift is as crucial as the gift itself; beautifully wrapping the item in decorative paper or fabric is essential, as it reflects the thoughtfulness behind the gesture. If you are fortunate enough to receive a gift, it is polite to express your heartfelt gratitude, and it is considered courteous to reciprocate with a gift of similar value at a later time. It is vital to remember that the act of giving should stem from genuine feelings, and the thoughtfulness behind the gift is what truly matters to the recipient.

Body Language

Body language in Japan can be quite different from what you might be accustomed to in your own culture. For instance, direct eye contact, which is often viewed as a sign of confidence and engagement in Western cultures, can be perceived as aggressive or disrespectful in Japan. Instead, a gentle gaze or looking slightly downward is considered more respectful and appropriate in social interactions. Moreover, pointing with your finger is generally avoided; instead, using your whole hand to gesture or directing the person's attention with an open hand is seen as more polite. Personal space is also valued, so maintaining a respectful distance during conversations is greatly appreciated, ensuring that both parties feel comfortable and at ease.

Another intriguing aspect of Japanese communication is the nuanced use of silence. In Japan, silence can possess deep meaning, often signifying contemplation, respect, or agreement. Therefore, don't feel pressured to fill pauses in conversation with unnecessary chatter; instead, embrace these moments as a natural and important part of the communication process. By allowing for pauses, you demonstrate patience and understanding, traits that are highly valued in Japanese culture.

By taking the time to understand these cultural nuances, you will find that your interactions in Japan become considerably more meaningful and respectful. Embracing these customs not only enriches your travel experience but also leaves a positive and lasting impression on the people you meet along your journey. So, as you embark on your exploration of this fascinating country, remember to bow graciously, give gifts thoughtfully, and be attuned to the subtleties of body language. These small yet significant gestures will open doors to deeper connections and provide you with a richer understanding of Japan's unique and vibrant culture, allowing you to engage with the local community in a way that is both respectful and rewarding.

● MOBILE APPS FOR TRANSLATION AND COMMUNICATION

As you embark on your journey through Japan, language might seem like a barrier, but fear not—technology is here to help. With a smartphone in hand, you can navigate the linguistic landscape with ease, thanks to a variety of mobile apps designed for translation and communication.

First up, **Google Translate** is a traveler's best friend. This app offers real-time translation for text, voice, and even images. Simply point your camera at a sign or menu, and watch as Japanese characters transform into your native language. For conversations, the voice feature is invaluable, allowing you to speak or type in your language and have it translated instantly into Japanese, and vice versa.

Another excellent tool is **iTranslate**, which provides similar capabilities with a user-friendly interface. It supports over 100 languages, including Japanese, and offers a handy offline mode—perfect for when you're exploring remote areas without internet access.

For those looking to learn a bit of Japanese on the go, **Duolingo** offers a fun and engaging way to pick up essential phrases. While it won't make you fluent overnight, it can certainly help you understand basic greetings and expressions, which can go a long way in enhancing your travel experience.

Lastly, don't overlook the power of LINE, Japan's most popular messaging app. Not only does it allow you to communicate with locals, but it also offers translation features within chats. Plus, it's a great way to stay connected with new friends you meet along your journey.

With these apps at your disposal, you'll find that language barriers become less daunting, allowing you to focus on enjoying the vibrant culture and breathtaking sights that Japan has to offer.

• DO'S AND DON'TS: AVOIDING COMMON TOURIST MISTAKES

Traveling to Japan is more than just a trip; it's an immersive adventure that offers the chance to dive into a culture where ancient customs and futuristic innovation coexist in perfect harmony. Japan has something for everyone—from its breathtaking natural landscapes and world-class cuisine to its deeply ingrained hospitality. Yet, to make the most out of a visit, understanding Japan's unique social etiquette and norms is key. Avoiding common pitfalls will ensure you're not only respectful but that your experience becomes more authentic and enjoyable. To help you fully embrace your journey, here are some tips to avoid missteps and enhance your overall travel experience.

Respecting Japan's Culture of Etiquette and Harmony

Respect for others and a desire for social harmony are central values in Japanese culture. The Japanese society functions on unwritten rules that prioritize group needs and public order, which can be quite different from Western norms. For instance, the concept of "wa," which means harmony, underlies Japanese etiquette and social interactions. Understanding this principle can help you see why certain behaviors—like speaking quietly in public and showing politeness to strangers—are so valued. This desire for harmony can be felt everywhere, from orderly queues for the train to the quiet atmosphere in public spaces.

One of the most common mistakes tourists make is not fully understanding the cultural etiquette surrounding Japan's sacred sites, particularly the numerous shrines and temples scattered across the country. These spiritual places are sanctuaries for prayer, meditation, and worship. When visiting a shrine, for example, it's customary to bow slightly upon entering as a gesture of respect. This small act signals a recognition of the sacredness of the space. At the purification fountain typically located near the entrance, cleanse your hands and mouth before proceeding. This ritual, known as "temizu," is an ancient practice meant to purify visitors and prepare them to enter a sacred place with a clear mind and spirit.

While walking within these serene spaces, keep your voice down and refrain from loud conversations. Japan's temples and shrines are places where locals and visitors alike come to find peace and connect with their spirituality. Any displays of affection, loud laughter, or disruptive behavior can be seen as a lack of respect for these revered sites. By observing these customs, you honor the traditions upheld within these ancient walls.

Navigating Public Transportation with Respect

Japan's public transportation system, especially the trains, is known for its punctuality, efficiency, and cleanliness. The country has one of the most reliable train networks in the world, but this high standard also relies on a set of unwritten guidelines that keep everything running smoothly. One of the most important rules to remember is to keep your phone on silent mode, known in Japanese as "manner mode." If you must take a call, move to a designated area or wait until you've exited the train, as loud conversations on public transportation are considered disrespectful to other passengers.

The train experience in Japan also involves an element of personal space and courtesy. If you're traveling with a backpack or large luggage, it's polite to place it on the overhead rack or hold it in front of you, especially during rush hour. Doing so not only creates more space but shows that you are considerate of others' comfort. In many cities, you'll notice marked lines on the ground indicating where passengers should stand and wait for the next train. Forming lines and waiting your turn to board is an integral part of maintaining the flow and order of Japan's transit systems, especially during peak commuting hours.

Dining Etiquette and the Art of Gratitude

Food is a vital part of Japanese culture, and the country takes pride in its culinary heritage. Dining out in Japan can be a wonderful cultural experience, but it's essential to be aware of certain customs and practices. Before starting your meal, it's customary to say "Itadakimasu," a phrase that translates to "I humbly receive." This simple expression of gratitude shows appreciation for the food and those who have prepared it. At the end of the meal, you can say "Gochisousama deshita," which means "thank you for the feast," to express gratitude once again.

Using chopsticks properly is another crucial aspect of dining etiquette in Japan. There are a few things to keep in mind. Firstly, avoid sticking your chopsticks upright in a bowl of rice, as this resembles a ritual done at funerals and is seen as disrespectful. If you need to put your chopsticks down, rest them neatly on the chopstick holder provided or across your bowl. Additionally, passing food from one person's chopsticks to another's is also frowned upon, as this action is reminiscent of funeral practices. Instead, place food on a small plate for the other person to take.

When dining out, tipping is not customary in Japan and is even considered rude in many establishments. If you want to show appreciation for excellent service, a simple thank you, or "Arigato gozaimasu," is more than sufficient. This gesture of respect aligns with the Japanese cultural ethos, where service is seen as a part of the job, and quality is expected without additional reward.

Bridging the Language Barrier

While many Japanese people, especially in urban areas, have some understanding of English, learning a few basic Japanese phrases can make a big difference in your interactions. Simple expressions like "Sumimasen" (excuse me) and "Arigato gozaimasu" (thank you very much) show respect and appreciation. Greeting someone with "Konnichiwa" (hello) or "Ohayo gozaimasu" (good morning) can create a positive first impression, signaling your openness to the culture. Japanese people often value effort in communication, so even a modest attempt to speak the language can be warmly received and can make your interactions more rewarding.

Pedestrian Etiquette and Respecting Personal Space

Japan's major cities are bustling, yet they maintain an impressive orderliness in pedestrian traffic. Whether you're wandering through the neon-lit streets of Shibuya or the historic districts of Kyoto, being mindful of your surroundings is essential. Walk on the left side of the sidewalk when possible, and observe how locals navigate the space. Avoid stopping suddenly in busy areas, as this can disrupt the flow of foot traffic. If you need to check directions or take photos, step aside to avoid inconveniencing others. Following the local flow and respecting shared spaces will make your urban explorations more enjoyable.

Exploring Off-the-Beaten-Path Locations

It can be tempting to stick to popular tourist sites, but venturing beyond these well-known attractions often provides the most memorable experiences. Japan is filled with hidden gems—whether it's a tranquil village with traditional wooden houses, a lesser-known temple surrounded by forest, or a quiet beach along the coast. These locations are often less crowded, allowing for a more immersive experience where you can connect with the landscape and people at a deeper level. Exploring beyond the typical tourist paths not only offers a fresh perspective but also fosters a genuine appreciation for Japan's local culture and way of life.

In addition to enhancing your travel experience, exploring lesser-known areas can also be beneficial for local communities that may not see as much tourist activity. When visiting these places, try to support local businesses by dining at family-owned restaurants, purchasing handmade crafts, or even staying in traditional guesthouses. This approach helps you contribute positively to the local economy while enjoying an authentic slice of Japan.

Preparing for Unexpected Cultural Differences

Japan has unique customs and norms that may be unfamiliar to first-time visitors. Public trash cans, for instance, are rare, so it's common to carry a small bag for disposing of your trash later. The practice of separating trash into categories (burnable, non-burnable, and recyclable) is also standard. Understanding these small differences beforehand can help you avoid any cultural missteps and contribute to keeping Japan's streets clean and orderly.

When it comes to bathing in Japan, public baths (onsen) and hot springs are a beloved tradition. If you decide to experience an onsen, be aware that there are specific rules: you must wash and rinse thoroughly before entering the communal bath. Most onsens require you to be fully naked, as swimsuits are generally not allowed, and tattoos may need to be covered in certain places due to cultural sensitivities.

Final Reflections: Embrace the Journey with a Respectful Heart

Traveling in Japan is a learning experience as much as it is a sightseeing journey. Each interaction, meal, and cultural practice offers a new perspective, broadening your understanding of what it means to be a respectful traveler. While each country has its own customs and ways of life, Japan's commitment to harmony, respect, and order can be incredibly rewarding to experience firsthand. By approaching your journey with an open mind, curiosity, and a respectful attitude, you'll be rewarded with deeper connections and memories that will stay with you long after you've left.

Traveling is about more than just seeing new places; it's about adapting, appreciating, and learning from the experiences you encounter. Embrace each aspect of Japan's vibrant culture, and you'll leave with a heart full of memories and perhaps a renewed sense of gratitude for the unique customs that make Japan such an extraordinary place.

ITINERARIES FOR EVERY TRAVELER

Imagine stepping off the train in Tokyo, the city that never seems to sleep, yet offers serene pockets of tranquility. For the urban explorer, begin your journey in Shibuya, where the famous crossing feels like a dance of humanity. Dive into the vibrant chaos of Harajuku, where fashion knows no bounds, before finding a moment of peace at the Meiji Shrine, nestled within a lush forest.

For those seeking a historical journey, Kyoto awaits. Wander through the Arashiyama Bamboo Grove, its towering stalks swaying gently in the breeze, a whisper of ancient times. The golden splendor of Kinkaku-ji reflects in the pond, a sight that feels like stepping into a painting. As evening falls, stroll through Gion, hoping to catch a glimpse of a geisha, a fleeting moment of the past.

In Osaka, the food lover finds paradise. The streets of Dotonbori are alive with the sizzle of takoyaki and the irresistible aroma of okonomiyaki. Let your taste buds guide you through this culinary wonderland, each bite a new discovery.

● 7-DAY ITINERARY: CLASSIC HIGHLIGHTS FOR FIRST-TIMERS

Welcome to your first journey through Japan, a land where ancient traditions blend seamlessly with cutting-edge modernity. As you embark on this 7-day adventure, you'll find yourself immersed in an enchanting world of vibrant cities, serene temples, and breathtaking landscapes. Let us guide you through a thoughtfully curated itinerary that captures the essence of Japan, ensuring your experience is both memorable and fulfilling.

Day 1: Tokyo - The Heartbeat of Japan

Your journey begins in Tokyo, a bustling metropolis that never sleeps. Upon arrival, embrace the city's energy by exploring the iconic Shibuya Crossing, where hundreds cross the street in a mesmerizing dance of humanity. From there, make your way to the historic Senso-ji Temple in Asakusa, where the scent of incense and the sound of temple bells transport you to another era. As the sun sets, head to the Tokyo Skytree for a panoramic view of the city's dazzling skyline, a perfect way to end your first day.

Day 2: Tokyo - Tradition Meets Innovation

Start your day in the tranquil Meiji Shrine, a spiritual oasis in the heart of the city. Stroll through the lush forested paths and partake in a traditional Shinto ritual. Next, dive into the quirky world of Harajuku, where fashion and creativity know no bounds. In the afternoon, visit the Akihabara district, a paradise for tech enthusiasts and anime fans alike. Conclude your Tokyo exploration in the historic district of Ginza, where you can indulge in fine dining and shopping.

Day 3: Hakone - Gateway to Mount Fuji

Leave the urban hustle behind as you travel to Hakone, a picturesque region renowned for its hot springs and views of Mount Fuji. Begin your exploration with a serene boat ride across Lake Ashi, followed by a visit to the Hakone Shrine, hidden amidst towering cedar trees. Take the Hakone Ropeway for a breathtaking view of the volcanic landscapes and the majestic Mount Fuji. End your day by soaking in an onsen, a traditional Japanese hot spring, to unwind and rejuvenate.

Day 4: Kyoto - The Cultural Capital

Travel to Kyoto, a city steeped in history and tradition. Your first stop should be the Fushimi Inari Taisha, famous for its thousands of vibrant red torii gates that create a mesmerizing path up the mountain.

Continue to the Kinkaku-ji (Golden Pavilion), where the shimmering gold leaf reflects beautifully on the surrounding pond. In the evening, wander through the historic streets of Gion, keeping an eye out for elusive geisha gliding gracefully to their appointments.

Day 5: Kyoto - Temples and Tea

Begin your day at the Arashiyama Bamboo Grove, where towering bamboo stalks sway gently in the breeze, creating an otherworldly atmosphere. Nearby, visit the Tenryu-ji Temple, a UNESCO World Heritage site with exquisite Zen gardens.

After lunch, partake in a traditional tea ceremony, a serene ritual that embodies the essence of Japanese culture. In the evening, explore the Nishiki Market, sampling local delicacies and shopping for unique souvenirs.

Day 6: Osaka - The Vibrant City

Head to Osaka, a city known for its lively atmosphere and culinary delights. Start your exploration at Osaka Castle, a symbol of the city's rich history. Next, dive into the bustling streets of Dotonbori, where neon lights and street food stalls create a feast for the senses. Be sure to try local specialties like takoyaki and okonomiyaki. In the evening, enjoy a leisurely stroll along the Umeda Sky Building's floating garden observatory, offering stunning views of the city.

Day 7: Nara - A Journey Back in Time

Conclude your journey with a day trip to Nara, Japan's first permanent capital. Visit the Todai-ji Temple, home to the Great Buddha, an awe-inspiring bronze statue. Wander through Nara Park, where friendly deer roam freely, adding a touch of magic to the experience. Before returning to Osaka for your departure, stop by the Kofuku-ji Temple and admire its historic pagodas. As you reflect on your adventures, cherish the memories of Japan's captivating blend of tradition and modernity.

This 7-day itinerary is designed to give you a taste of Japan's diverse offerings, from bustling cities to serene landscapes. As you journey through this remarkable country, embrace each moment with an open heart and mind, and let the spirit of Japan leave an indelible mark on your soul.

Travel Tips for Backpackers:

- **Meals**: Take advantage of Japan's convenience stores for affordable yet delicious food options like onigiri, sandwiches, and bento boxes. For hot meals, seek out ramen, udon, or small eateries offering "teishoku" (set meals).
- **Accommodations**: Budget hostels, capsule hotels, and guesthouses are widely available in all major cities. Book in advance, especially in popular tourist spots.
- **Etiquette**: Always respect local customs—bow when greeting, avoid loud conversations in public spaces, and follow strict recycling rules when disposing of waste.
- **Packing**: Pack light and include essentials like a portable charger, refillable water bottle, lightweight rain jacket, comfortable shoes for walking, and a small daypack for day trips.

• 10-Day Spiritual Journey Across Japan's Lesser-Known Islands: Shikoku and Yakushima

Welcome to a unique 10-day adventure exploring the spiritual heart of Japan through two of its less-visited islands, Shikoku and Yakushima. Known for their deeply rooted sacred traditions, ancient temples, and untouched natural beauty, these islands offer an authentic glimpse into Japan's spiritual heritage, far from the crowds of popular tourist destinations. This itinerary is designed for those who seek not only to discover temples and monasteries but also to connect with the local culture, living simply, and traveling light.

Day 1-2: Arriving in Shikoku - Tokushima and the Sacred Pilgrimage

Day 1: Tokushima - Gateway to the Pilgrimage
Your journey begins on the island of **Shikoku**, famed for the **Shikoku Pilgrimage (Ohenro)**, a 1,200-kilometer route that circles the island, visiting 88 temples. Begin your pilgrimage at **Ryozenji Temple**, the first on the route, located in **Naruto City** in Tokushima Prefecture. Here, you'll receive a pilgrim's white vest (hakui) and walking staff (kongō-zue), symbols of the spiritual journey.

After visiting **Gokurakuji Temple** (the second on the pilgrimage), take time to explore the quiet countryside around Naruto. Enjoy a simple dinner at a local ryokan, sampling traditional vegetarian Buddhist cuisine known as **shojin ryori**. Stay overnight in a temple lodging (shukubo) for an immersive experience. Shukubo often provides basic accommodations with communal baths, ideal for budget travelers seeking an authentic stay.

Day 2: Tokushima - Temples and Nature
Start your day with a meditative hike up **Mount Bizan**, offering panoramic views of Tokushima City and surrounding areas. The mountain is a symbol of Tokushima, and at its peak, you'll find **Bizan Temple**, an often-overlooked treasure with a peaceful atmosphere.

Spend the afternoon exploring **Konsen-ji Temple** (the third on the pilgrimage), nestled among lush greenery. Enjoy the serenity of the temple grounds, which offer a chance for quiet reflection.

For meals, explore Tokushima's local food scene. Try the famous **Tokushima ramen**, a hearty dish perfect for travelers. Budget travelers will find affordable accommodations in small guesthouses (minshuku) or even hostels around Tokushima.

Day 3-5: Kochi - Sacred Temples and Coastal Beauty

Day 3: Kochi City - Temples and Castles Travel to **Kochi City**, home to some of the most beautiful temples on the pilgrimage. Begin with **Chikurin-ji Temple** (number 31 on the pilgrimage), perched on a hilltop overlooking the city. This temple is renowned for its pagoda and tranquil gardens.

Afterward, visit **Kochi Castle**, one of Japan's 12 original castles, and spend your afternoon wandering through the old merchant district, where you can find traditional handicrafts and enjoy fresh seafood from Kochi's famous **Hirome Market**. Kochi also offers budget hostels and guesthouses near the city center.

Day 4: Cape Muroto - Sacred Mountain Retreats On this day, journey to **Cape Muroto**, where temples such as **Hotsumisakiji Temple** (number 24) provide a spiritual retreat amidst stunning coastal scenery. Cape Muroto is a UNESCO Geopark with dramatic cliffs and rugged beauty, perfect for reflective walks along the coast.

Stay overnight in a small temple lodging, offering simple meals and the opportunity to join the monks in early morning prayers. This is an excellent opportunity to experience the slower pace of life in rural Japan. For backpackers, camping by the coast is also an option, with affordable campsites nearby.

Day 5: Kochi - River and Temples
Return to Kochi City, stopping at **Sekkei-ji Temple**, which has deep historical ties to the introduction of Zen Buddhism in Japan. In the afternoon, take a relaxing boat trip along the **Shimanto River**, considered one of Japan's last clear rivers.

This is a great time to enjoy some local food, such as **katsuo no tataki** (seared bonito), a regional specialty, in one of the riverside restaurants. Spend the night in Kochi at a local guesthouse or cheap ryokan for another authentic experience.

Day 6-7: Yakushima - Island of Ancient Forests and Sacred Sites

Day 6: Arrival in Yakushima - Mystical Forests
Fly or ferry to the mystical island of **Yakushima**, a UNESCO World Heritage Site renowned for its ancient cedar forests and spiritual significance. Upon arrival, settle into one of the local guesthouses or **backpacker hostels**, which offer budget-friendly options in the island's small villages.

In the afternoon, explore **Shitogo Gajumaru Tree Forest**, a lesser-known area where giant banyan trees dominate the landscape, creating an almost otherworldly atmosphere. This is the perfect introduction to Yakushima's untouched natural beauty.

Day 7: Yakusugi Land - Walking Among the Ancients
Begin your day with a hike through **Yakusugi Land**, a pristine

area of ancient cedar trees, some over 2,000 years old. Among them is **Jomon Sugi**, the oldest and most sacred tree in Japan. This hike offers both short and long trails, making it accessible to various fitness levels.

Yakushima is also known for its stunning waterfalls, so don't miss **Senpirono Falls** or **Oko-no-taki Waterfall**, both offering peaceful spots for reflection. In the evening, enjoy a simple dinner of local fish and vegetables, before relaxing in a traditional guesthouse.

For the budget-conscious, Yakushima offers free public onsen (hot springs) where travelers can unwind after a day of hiking.

Day 8-10: Yakushima's Sacred Trails and Hidden Temples

Day 8: Shiratani Unsuikyo Ravine - Path to Spiritual Reflection

Today, explore **Shiratani Unsuikyo Ravine**, a moss-covered forest that feels like stepping into a fairytale. This ancient forest inspired the setting for Studio Ghibli's "Princess Mononoke." The peaceful paths here are perfect for contemplative walks, where you can reflect on your journey.

Pack a lunch and enjoy a picnic at one of the lookout points, where you'll be treated to breathtaking views of the island's mountains. For a more immersive experience, consider spending the night camping in designated areas within the park. Yakushima's campsites are well-maintained and offer a budget-friendly option for nature lovers.

Day 9: Temples and Traditions

Spend this day visiting Yakushima's smaller temples, such as the **Yakushima Lighthouse Shrine**, a hidden gem seldom visited by tourists. Here, you can participate in a traditional prayer ceremony with the local priest, offering a deeper understanding of the island's spiritual heritage.

Visit the local village markets to sample **flying fish**, a Yakushima specialty, and learn more about the island's sustainable living practices. For accommodation, stay in a traditional homestay (minpaku) where you can interact with locals and enjoy home-cooked meals.

Day 10: Departure and Reflection

On your final day, take a quiet morning walk along Yakushima's secluded beaches, such as **Isso Beach**, known for its crystal-clear waters and serene atmosphere. Reflect on your journey through the spiritual landscapes of Shikoku and Yakushima, feeling the deep connection between nature and spirituality that defines these islands.

Before departing, enjoy a final meal of local specialties at a small restaurant near the port or airport, celebrating the culmination of your 10-day adventure.

Travel Tips for Backpackers:

Meals:

Opt for affordable local food options like **Tokushima ramen** in Tokushima, and **katsuo no tataki** (seared bonito) in Kochi. Markets like **Hirome Market** in Kochi offer a variety of budget-friendly meals, while small restaurants near Yakushima's port serve fresh local fish. For a more spiritual experience, try **shojin ryori** (Buddhist vegetarian cuisine) when staying at temple lodgings (shukubo). Convenience stores (konbini) are also an excellent option for inexpensive yet delicious meals, especially for travelers on the go.

Accommodations:

For an immersive experience, stay in **shukubo** (temple lodgings), which offer simple, affordable rooms often shared with other travelers. In cities like Tokushima and Kochi, **guesthouses** (minshuku) and hostels provide budget options with communal spaces. For nature lovers in Yakushima, **campsites** in national parks or designated camping areas are an excellent low-cost option. Be sure to book ahead, especially during peak travel seasons.

Etiquette:

When visiting temples, dress modestly and follow local customs, such as removing your shoes before entering sacred spaces. Always remain quiet and respectful, especially during prayer times or meditative hikes. It's also important to be mindful of Japan's recycling rules when camping, and to clean up after yourself in public spaces. When staying in homestays (minpaku), show gratitude by learning a few basic phrases in Japanese, and always be respectful of your host's home.

Packing:

Pack light and prioritize comfortable walking shoes, as much of this journey involves hiking and walking through forest trails. Bring weather-appropriate clothing, such as a **rain jacket** for Yakushima, which is known for frequent rain. A reusable water bottle and a small daypack are essential for hiking, while a **quick-dry towel** and a portable power bank will be useful for both city and countryside travel. If you're camping, bring basic camping gear, but know that many campsites offer simple facilities.

● 14-DAY ITINERARY: EXPLORING JAPAN'S DEPTH AND DIVERSITY

Embarking on a 14-day journey across Japan offers a rich tapestry of experiences that beautifully encapsulate the country's unique blend of tradition and modernity. From the bustling streets of Tokyo, where the future is on display, to the tranquil temples of Kyoto that whisper ancient stories, this itinerary is meticulously designed to guide you through some of Japan's most iconic locations while also revealing hidden gems that promise an authentic taste of the nation's culture and traditions. Each day brings new adventures, culinary delights, and opportunities for deep reflection, making your time in Japan an unforgettable experience.

Day 1-3: Tokyo - The Heartbeat of Modern Japan

Begin your adventure in Tokyo, a sprawling metropolis where futuristic skyscrapers stand proudly alongside historic temples, creating a fascinating contrast that defines the city. Start with a visit to the Asakusa district, where the iconic Senso-ji Temple awaits. This sacred site, the oldest temple in Tokyo, offers an immersive experience, as the air is filled with the scent of incense and the vibrant energy of visitors from around the globe. Stroll down Nakamise Street, a bustling pathway lined with stalls selling traditional snacks like freshly made melon bread and ningyo-yaki, alongside charming souvenirs that make for perfect mementos of your visit.

In the afternoon, take a tranquil walk to the Meiji Shrine, a peaceful oasis amid the city's hustle and bustle. The shrine, dedicated to Emperor Meiji and Empress Shoken, is surrounded by a lush forest, creating a serene atmosphere perfect for contemplation. If you're fortunate, you might even witness a traditional Shinto wedding ceremony taking place in the beautiful outdoor setting.

When evening descends, immerse yourself in the vibrant nightlife of Shibuya and Shinjuku. Here, the neon lights and lively crowds create an electrifying atmosphere. Make sure to experience the iconic Shibuya Crossing, where hundreds of people flow together, crossing the intersection in a mesmerizing dance that epitomizes Tokyo's energy.

Day 4-5: Nikko - A Step into Nature and History

On Day 4, take a day trip to Nikko, a UNESCO World Heritage site that beautifully combines natural beauty with historical significance. Visit the opulent Toshogu Shrine, the lavish mausoleum of Tokugawa Ieyasu, the founder of the Tokugawa shogunate. The shrine's intricate carvings and vibrant colors are a feast for the eyes, reflecting the craftsmanship and artistry of the Edo period. As you wander through the grounds, take time to appreciate the tranquil setting and the ornate buildings that tell the story of Japan's feudal era.

In addition to the shrines, explore the breathtaking natural wonders of Nikko National Park. Walk through serene forests where towering trees stand sentinel, and visit the stunning Kegon Falls, one of Japan's most famous waterfalls. The cascade plummets 97 meters into Lake Chuzenji below, and it is particularly enchanting in autumn when the leaves turn vibrant shades of red, orange, and gold, creating a truly picturesque scene.

Day 6-8: Kyoto - The Cultural Capital

Travel to Kyoto, a city that embodies the spirit of traditional Japan and is often referred to as the cultural heart of the country. Begin your exploration in the Arashiyama district, where you can wander through the enchanting Bamboo Grove, an otherworldly path flanked by towering bamboo stalks that sway gently in the breeze. Beyond the grove, visit the Iwatayama Monkey Park, where you can interact with wild monkeys in their natural habitat, offering a unique experience that is both fun and educational.

Immerse yourself in history at the breathtaking Kinkaku-ji, also known as the Golden Pavilion, which glimmers atop a reflecting pond, surrounded by meticulously curated gardens that change with the seasons. Then, head to Ryoan-ji, famous for its Zen rock garden, where you can find a moment of tranquility as you contemplate its simple yet profound design. In the afternoon, delve into the Gion district, renowned for its well-preserved wooden machiya houses and the chance to spot a geisha gracefully making her way to an evening appointment. The air is filled with a palpable sense of history and elegance as you stroll the cobbled streets.

On your last day in Kyoto, do not miss visiting the Fushimi Inari Shrine, celebrated for its thousands of vermillion-red torii gates that create a mesmerizing path up the sacred Inari Mountain. As you hike through the gates, you will be enveloped in a mystical ambiance that is quintessentially Japanese. Each gate, donated by individuals and businesses, tells a story of gratitude to the kami that protects the region.

Day 9: Nara - Ancient Temples and Free-Roaming Deer

A short train ride from Kyoto brings you to Nara, the birthplace of Japanese civilization and home to some of the country's oldest temples. Explore the tranquil Nara Park, where friendly deer roam freely, adding to the picturesque setting. Visit the majestic Todai-ji Temple, housing the Great Buddha, a colossal bronze statue that stands as a remarkable feat of ancient engineering and artistry. The sheer size and beauty of this statue will leave you in awe.

As you wander through the park, take the opportunity to interact with the gentle deer, considered sacred and recognized as a symbol of the city. Feel the joy as they approach for a treat or simply stroll by your side. Conclude your day with a visit to Kasuga-taisha Shrine, known for its hundreds of bronze lanterns that illuminate the pathways, creating an ethereal atmosphere, especially at dusk when the lanterns are lit.

Day 10-11: Osaka - Culinary Delights and Vibrant Streets

Your next destination is Osaka, a city renowned for its vibrant food culture and lively atmosphere. Begin your culinary adventure in the bustling Dotonbori district, where the tantalizing aromas of local specialties like takoyaki (octopus balls) and okonomiyaki (savory pancakes) fill the air. Experience the vibrant energy as you dine al fresco along the canal, illuminated by neon lights and the giant billboards that tower above, creating an unforgettable dining experience.

After indulging in the local cuisine, visit the historic Osaka Castle, a stunning landmark surrounded by beautiful gardens. Explore its rich history and enjoy panoramic views of the city from the top floor. In the evening, ascend the Umeda Sky Building for breathtaking views of the sprawling metropolis, particularly stunning at sunset when the city lights begin to twinkle like stars.

Day 12: Hiroshima and Miyajima - A Journey of Reflection

On Day 12, travel to Hiroshima, a city that embodies resilience and hope. Spend the morning at the Peace Memorial Park and Museum, a poignant reminder of the city's tragic past. As you walk through the park, you will encounter the haunting remnants of Hiroshima's history, including the iconic Atomic Bomb Dome, which serves as a symbol of peace and a testament to the city's recovery. The museum provides a thought-provoking insight into the events of August 6, 1945, inviting reflection and a deeper understanding of the value of peace.

In the afternoon, take a ferry to nearby Miyajima Island to see the world-renowned Itsukushima Shrine and its floating torii gate. As the sun begins to set, the torii gate appears to float on the water, creating a breathtaking view that has captivated visitors for centuries. Explore the charming streets of Miyajima, sampling local delicacies like grilled oyster and momiji manju (maple leaf-shaped cakes), before returning to Hiroshima for the night.

Day 13: Himeji - The Majestic White Heron Castle

On your way back to Tokyo, make a stop in Himeji to visit the stunning Himeji Castle, often referred to as the White Heron Castle due to its elegant, white appearance that resembles a bird taking flight. As you explore this UNESCO World Heritage site, you'll be transported back to Japan's feudal past, with its well-preserved structures and intricate defensive systems.

Stroll through the surrounding landscaped gardens, where cherry blossoms bloom in spring and vibrant foliage paints a picture in autumn, offering a serene retreat before continuing your journey.

Day 14: Return to Tokyo - Final Reflections

Conclude your incredible journey in Tokyo, where you can revisit your favorite spots or explore new areas like the trendy Harajuku district, known for its eclectic fashion scene and youth culture, or the tranquil Imperial Palace grounds, a peaceful escape in the heart of the city.

As you reflect on the diverse experiences, from the vibrant urban landscapes to the serene countryside, you'll find that each location has left an indelible mark on your heart.

As you prepare to depart, take a moment to appreciate the warmth of Japanese hospitality, the breathtaking landscapes, and the rich cultural tapestry that defines this remarkable country. Japan, a land that seamlessly blends the past with the present, has offered you an unforgettable experience filled with memories that will last a lifetime.

Travel Tips for Backpackers:

Embarking on this 14-day journey across Japan promises both thrilling adventures and serene moments of reflection. To make the most of your backpacking experience, here are some practical tips to keep your trip budget-friendly, immersive, and enjoyable.

Meals:

- **Convenience Stores (Konbini)**: Japan's convenience stores (like 7-Eleven, FamilyMart, and Lawson) offer a wide variety of delicious and affordable meals. You can grab onigiri (rice balls), bento boxes, and fresh sandwiches for around ¥300-¥600.

- **Street Food**: In areas like Osaka's **Dotonbori** or Tokyo's **Asakusa**, indulge in local street foods such as **takoyaki** (octopus balls) and **okonomiyaki** (savory pancakes). These are not only tasty but also affordable, with prices ranging from ¥500-¥800.

- **Local Ramen and Udon Shops**: Small, local ramen or udon shops are perfect for budget travelers. Meals typically cost ¥500-¥1000 and offer a hearty, authentic experience.

- **Soba and Gyudon Chains**: Budget-friendly restaurant chains like **Matsuya**, **Sukiya**, or **Yoshinoya** serve Japanese comfort food, like **gyudon** (beef bowls), starting at ¥300-¥500.

Accommodations:

- **Hostels and Capsule Hotels**: Throughout Japan, hostels and capsule hotels offer clean and affordable lodging for backpackers, ranging from ¥2,000-¥5,000 per night. These are available in major cities like Tokyo, Kyoto, and Osaka, as well as smaller cities like Nikko and Hiroshima.

- **Guesthouses (Minshuku)**: For a more traditional experience, stay at **minshuku** (Japanese guesthouses). These are typically family-run and offer basic amenities at affordable rates (around ¥3,000-¥6,000 per night). Meals may be included for an additional charge.

- **Temple Lodging (Shukubo)**: In places like Kyoto or Nikko, you can experience **shukubo**, staying overnight in a temple for around ¥5,000-¥10,000 per night. This often includes the opportunity to participate in morning prayers or meditations.

- **Couchsurfing and Airbnbs**: Consider **Couchsurfing** or affordable Airbnbs for a more personal, local experience. This also allows you to connect with locals who can provide insights into their culture.

Etiquette:

- **Shoes Off Indoors**: Always remove your shoes when entering someone's home, traditional accommodations (like ryokan or minshuku), or certain temples and shrines.

- **Quiet in Public Spaces**: Japan values quiet and respect in public areas, especially in temples and shrines. Keep your voice low and be mindful of your surroundings.

- **Tipping**: Tipping is not customary in Japan and can even be seen as rude. Instead, express gratitude with a polite bow or verbal thanks.

- **Respect Sacred Spaces**: In temples, shrines, and religious ceremonies, be respectful by following local customs, such as bowing before entering a shrine or washing your hands at the purification fountain.

Packing:

- **Portable Wifi or SIM Card**: Japan is highly connected, and having access to maps and translations on the go is essential for backpackers. Portable Wi-Fi devices or local SIM cards can be rented or purchased at airports or electronics stores.

- **Comfortable Walking Shoes**: Japan's cities are best explored on foot, and places like Kyoto's Fushimi Inari Shrine and Yakushima's trails require comfortable, sturdy shoes.

- **Travel Light**: Opt for a lightweight backpack with versatile clothing for different weather conditions. In October to April, pack layers, as evenings can get chilly, especially in places like Nikko and Kyoto.

- **Reusable Bottle**: Japan has public water fountains, and you can refill a bottle to save money and reduce plastic waste. Plus, vending machines are ubiquitous if you need a quick drink on the go.

- **Portable Charger**: Japan's train rides and long walks mean you'll be on the go for hours. Having a portable charger ensures your devices remain powered up, especially for navigation and photography.

By following these travel tips, you'll not only make your trip more affordable but also more immersive, allowing you to experience Japan's depth and diversity with a true backpacker's spirit.

• SPECIAL INTEREST ITINERARIES: FOOD LOVERS, HISTORY BUFFS AND ADVENTURE SEEKERS

Imagine strolling through the bustling streets of Tokyo, your senses bombarded by the vibrant colors and tantalizing aromas wafting from every corner. For food lovers, Japan is nothing short of a culinary paradise, offering a smorgasbord of flavors and textures that delight the palate and ignite the imagination. Start your journey at the famed Tsukiji Outer Market, a haven for seafood enthusiasts and culinary explorers alike, where you can sample incredibly fresh sushi and sashimi while learning about the intricate art of fish preparation from knowledgeable local vendors who are eager to share their expertise.

The market's lively atmosphere, filled with the chatter of vendors and the clatter of bamboo steamers, invites you to try delicacies such as grilled eel, sea urchin, and even unique treats like sushi burritos. Venture into the hidden alleys of Osaka, known affectionately as the 'Nation's Kitchen,' where you can indulge in street food delights like takoyaki—crispy dough balls filled with tender octopus—and okonomiyaki, savory pancakes packed with toppings that vary from seafood to vegetables. The experience is not just about tasting; it's about connecting with the region's rich culinary heritage, where every dish tells a story of tradition and innovation. Take your time to sit at a bustling food stall, watching skilled chefs work their magic while enjoying a local beer or sake to truly immerse yourself in the vibrant food culture.

For those with a penchant for history, Japan offers a rich tapestry of stories woven through its ancient temples and shrines, each site revealing the profound spirituality and cultural significance that shapes the nation. Begin your historical journey in Kyoto, the heart of traditional Japan, where the serene beauty of Kinkaku-ji, the Golden Pavilion, surrounded by lush gardens and tranquil ponds, will transport you back to the days of the shogun. The shimmering gold leaf that adorns the structure reflects perfectly in the water, creating a scene that seems almost otherworldly. Wander through the historic streets of Gion, where the whispers of geisha still echo through elegant wooden teahouses, and you may even catch a glimpse of these graceful women adorned in exquisite kimonos, skillfully navigating their way to evening appointments.

In Hiroshima, stand in solemn reflection at the Peace Memorial Park, a poignant reminder of the past and a symbol of hope for the future. The haunting presence of the Atomic Bomb Dome serves as a powerful landmark, challenging visitors to reflect on the resilience and spirit of the Japanese people. Each step through these hallowed sites is not just a walk through history; it is a journey that enriches your understanding of humanity's struggles and triumphs.

For the adventure seekers among you, Japan's diverse landscapes offer a playground of possibilities that cater to every thrill-seeker's desires. Scale the majestic heights of Mount Fuji, Japan's iconic peak, where the panoramic views from the summit are a well-deserved reward for the soul after a challenging ascent. As you gaze across the sprawling landscape below, framed by clouds and valleys, you will find a sense of accomplishment that is both invigorating and humbling. In the winter months, the powdery slopes of Hokkaido beckon with some of the best skiing and snowboarding in the world, drawing enthusiasts from all corners of the globe to experience the thrill of gliding down pristine runs surrounded by breathtaking natural beauty.

For a more tranquil experience, consider kayaking through the crystal-clear waters of Okinawa, where the vibrant coral reefs teem with marine life, inviting you to explore an underwater paradise teeming with colorful fish and exotic sea creatures. Whether you're soaring through the air on a paragliding adventure or diving into the depths of the ocean, Japan's natural wonders promise an adventure of a lifetime, filled with unforgettable moments and breathtaking scenery.

As you embark on these special interest itineraries, remember that Japan is a land of contrasts, where ancient traditions coexist harmoniously with cutting-edge innovation. Whether you're savoring the umami of a perfectly crafted bowl of ramen in a cozy, family-owned eatery or tracing the footsteps of samurai through the intricately designed halls of a centuries-old castle, each experience offers a unique glimpse into the soul of this remarkable country. With every taste, every story, and every adventure, you'll find yourself falling deeper in love with Japan—a place where every journey is a discovery waiting to unfold and every moment is a memory in the making. So lace up your walking shoes, gather your sense of wonder, and prepare to embark on an unforgettable journey through the enchanting landscapes of Japan, where the past and present intertwine to create a vibrant tapestry that is sure to leave an indelible mark on your heart.

• CUSTOMIZABLE ITINERARIES FOR UNIQUE TRAVEL EXPERIENCES

Imagine stepping off the plane, the air thick with excitement and the aroma of unfamiliar delicacies wafting through the terminal. Japan awaits, a land where tradition and modernity dance in perfect harmony. As you embark on this journey, consider crafting an itinerary that's as unique as your own travel aspirations. Whether you're drawn to the bustling streets of Tokyo or the serene temples of Kyoto, the key to an unforgettable experience lies in customizing your adventure to suit your interests.

Begin your exploration in Tokyo, a city that dazzles with its neon lights and endless energy. For those who thrive in the midst of urban chaos, spend your days wandering through the vibrant districts of Shibuya and Shinjuku. But Tokyo is not just about its futuristic skyline; it offers pockets of tranquility in places like Meiji Shrine, where you can find a moment of peace amidst the city's hustle. Don't forget to indulge in the culinary delights of Tsukiji Outer Market, where fresh sushi and local treats await.

If your heart yearns for a glimpse into Japan's imperial past, Kyoto is your next stop. Here, the ancient capital unfolds with its stunning array of temples, gardens, and traditional tea houses. Customize your time by visiting the iconic Fushimi Inari Shrine, with its thousands of torii gates, or take a leisurely stroll through the Arashiyama Bamboo Grove. For a truly unique experience, consider participating in a traditional tea ceremony, immersing yourself in the serenity and precision of this age-old practice.

For those seeking a blend of modern and traditional, Osaka offers a vibrant culinary scene and a welcoming atmosphere. Known as the "Kitchen of Japan," Osaka is a food lover's paradise. Customize your visit by exploring Dotonbori, where street food stalls tempt you with takoyaki and okonomiyaki. To balance the urban excitement, spend an afternoon at Osaka Castle, where history and nature converge beautifully.

Beyond the well-trodden paths of these major cities, Japan offers countless hidden gems that promise a more intimate experience. Venture to the lesser-known town of Takayama, nestled in the Japanese Alps. Here, you can wander through well-preserved Edo-period streets and savor the local Hida beef. Alternatively, explore the island of Shikoku, where the pilgrimage route of 88 temples offers a spiritual journey through breathtaking landscapes.

As you plan your journey, remember that the beauty of Japan lies not only in its destinations but in the serendipitous moments that happen along the way. Allow yourself the freedom to deviate from your itinerary, to follow a local's recommendation for a family-run ramen shop or to linger a little longer in a place that speaks to your soul. These unplanned adventures often lead to the most cherished memories.

Lastly, embrace the cultural nuances that make Japan so special. Whether it's learning a few basic phrases in Japanese to connect with locals or understanding the etiquette of bowing, these small gestures of respect enhance your travel experience and deepen your connection to the country.

In crafting your itinerary, let your interests and curiosities guide you. Whether you're drawn to the vibrant cityscapes, the tranquil countryside, or the rich cultural heritage, Japan offers a tapestry of experiences waiting to be discovered. With a customized itinerary, your journey through the Land of the Rising Sun will be as unique and unforgettable as you are.

MAGIC TIPS FOR VISITING JAPAN FROM NORTH TO SOUTH (WHAT TO DO AND NOT TO DO)

As you embark on your journey through Japan, from the snow-capped peaks of Hokkaido to the sun-drenched beaches of Okinawa, it's essential to embrace both the etiquette and the spirit of this enchanting land. Imagine starting your day in Tokyo, the city that never sleeps, where the morning rush is a symphony of organized chaos. Here, standing on the correct side of the escalator is not just a courtesy; it's a dance of respect among commuters. As you navigate the bustling streets, remember that a simple bow can open doors to a world of warmth and hospitality.

Heading south, Kyoto awaits with its serene temples and whispering bamboo groves. In this city of tradition, let the quiet elegance of a tea ceremony transport you to another time. As you savor each sip, know that your presence in this ritual is a bridge between cultures, a moment where time stands still.

Further along, Osaka's vibrant energy will pull you into its culinary embrace. Here, the streets are alive with the sizzling sounds of takoyaki stands and the laughter of people enjoying life's simple pleasures. Embrace the local saying, "kuidaore," or "eat until you drop," and indulge in the city's gastronomic wonders.

Finally, as you reach the southern islands, let the tranquil beauty of Okinawa's beaches remind you of the importance of balance. Here, the pace slows, and the rhythm of life is dictated by the ebb and flow of the ocean. Take a moment to breathe, to reflect, and to appreciate the journey you've undertaken.

Throughout your travels, remember that Japan is a land of contrasts, where the ancient and the modern coexist in harmony. By respecting its customs and embracing its diversity, you will not only discover the beauty of the country but also the warmth of its people. Let your journey be guided by curiosity and respect, and Japan will reveal its magic to you in ways unimaginable.

• TOKYO AND KANTO REGION

The Kanto region is the political, economic, and cultural heart of Japan, home to the bustling metropolis of Tokyo and surrounding prefectures like Kanagawa, Chiba, Saitama, Ibaraki, Tochigi, and Gunma. Each of these areas offers unique experiences, blending the ultramodern with the traditional. Tokyo itself is a sprawling city that never sleeps, where neon lights, ancient temples, Michelin-starred restaurants, and cutting-edge technology coexist harmoniously. Beyond Tokyo, the Kanto region is home to serene coastal towns, mountainous retreats, and tranquil countryside landscapes. In this chapter, we'll explore the must-visit attractions in Tokyo, hidden gems in the Kanto region, local events, and give you practical advice on how to enjoy your trip to the fullest.

Discovering Tokyo

Tokyo is often the first stop for many travelers to Japan, and it offers a mind-boggling variety of things to see and do. Begin your journey in the historic district of Asakusa, where the famous Senso-ji Temple stands. This iconic temple is the oldest in Tokyo and a significant spiritual site for locals. Surrounding the temple is Nakamise Street, a lively shopping area where you can find traditional snacks and souvenirs.

For modern contrasts, head to the bustling district of Shibuya, known for the world-famous Shibuya Crossing, one of the busiest pedestrian intersections in the world. This is where Tokyo's energy is most palpable. Don't miss the trendy shopping streets of Harajuku, where fashion-forward youth culture thrives, or the skyscrapers of Shinjuku, where you can catch a stunning panoramic view of the city from the top of the Tokyo Metropolitan Government Building for free.

Tokyo is also a city of green spaces, and no visit is complete without strolling through Ueno Park, home to numerous museums and the Ueno Zoo, or the serene Meiji Shrine, located in a forested area in the heart of the city.

What to Do in Tokyo

Tokyo offers something for every type of traveler. For art and history enthusiasts, the Tokyo National Museum in Ueno is a treasure trove of artifacts, while the Edo-Tokyo Museum in Ryogoku offers insight into Tokyo's past. For anime and pop culture fans, Akihabara is a must-visit, with shops dedicated to manga, electronics, and gaming.

For a quieter experience, visit the Nezu Shrine, a lesser-known but beautiful shrine in Bunkyo Ward, where traditional wooden architecture blends with nature. It's an excellent spot to escape the crowds and enjoy a peaceful walk through the vermillion torii gates.

If you're interested in sumo wrestling, Ryogoku is the heart of sumo culture in Tokyo, and you can even catch a live sumo tournament at the Ryogoku Kokugikan arena if your timing is right.

What Events to Enjoy in Tokyo and Around

Tokyo hosts an array of festivals throughout the year. In spring, don't miss the Sakura Matsuri (Cherry Blossom Festival), particularly in Ueno Park or along the Meguro River, where cherry blossoms light up the sky in hues of pink and white.

In the summer, Tokyo comes alive with fireworks displays, the most famous being the Sumida River Fireworks Festival, held in July. Autumn brings the Meiji Jingu Gaien Ginkgo Festival, where the streets are lined with vibrant yellow ginkgo trees, offering a picturesque view of the changing seasons.

Winter is a magical time in Tokyo as well, with the Tokyo Midtown Christmas Illumination lighting up the city, and the traditional New Year's Day visit to temples and shrines, such as Zojo-ji and Meiji Shrine, to make your first prayers of the year.

What to Do in the Kanto Region

Beyond Tokyo, the Kanto region offers plenty of day trips and excursions. One popular destination is Kamakura, a coastal city known for its great Daibutsu (Great Buddha) and serene temples like Hasedera. Kamakura's scenic hiking trails provide a great escape from the city, and its beaches are perfect for relaxing in the warmer months.

For a more off-the-beaten-path experience, head to Nikko, in Tochigi Prefecture. Nikko National Park is a UNESCO World Heritage site, known for its stunning temples and shrines, including

Toshogu Shrine, dedicated to Tokugawa Ieyasu, the founder of the Tokugawa shogunate. Lake Chuzenji and Kegon Falls are natural wonders worth visiting, especially during the autumn foliage season.

Hakone, located in Kanagawa Prefecture, is another favorite spot, especially for those looking to relax in onsen (hot springs) while enjoying views of Mount Fuji. The Hakone Open-Air Museum is a unique attraction, combining art and nature in a beautiful setting.

For a more secluded experience, visit the Ogasawara Islands, a remote archipelago that can only be accessed by ferry from Tokyo. These islands are known for their unspoiled nature, rich marine life, and opportunities for diving and whale watching. It's a hidden gem that few tourists know about.

Where to Eat in Tokyo and the Kanto Region

Tokyo is a paradise for food lovers, from Michelin-starred restaurants to street food stalls. Start with the iconic Tsukiji Outer Market, where you can sample fresh sushi, grilled eel, and street snacks like tamagoyaki (Japanese omelet). For a more modern dining experience, visit Shibuya Sky for rooftop dining with panoramic views of the city.

In Yokohama, just outside Tokyo, you'll find Chinatown, which offers a fusion of Japanese and Chinese flavors. Be sure to try steamed buns filled with savory pork, known as nikuman, and sweet almond jelly for dessert.

For those venturing into Gunma Prefecture, the Tomioka Silk Mill is not only a UNESCO World Heritage site but also offers traditional local cuisine. Try konnyaku, a jelly-like dish made from the konjac plant, a specialty of the region.

What to Eat in Tokyo and the Kanto Region

Japanese cuisine in Kanto is diverse and flavorful. Sushi and ramen are must-tries, with numerous varieties available in every district of Tokyo. For ramen, visit Ichiran or Ippudo, two well-known chains, or explore the tiny ramen shops in Shinjuku or Akihabara for more unique offerings.

In Kawagoe, also known as "Little Edo," enjoy traditional sweet potato treats like imo yokan and sweet potato ice cream, which are specialties of the area.

For something truly unique, head to Chichibu, where you can taste miso potato—deep-fried potato skewers dipped in miso sauce, a comforting and savory street food.

Where to Stay in Tokyo and the Kanto Region

Tokyo has accommodations for every budget. In the upscale district of Ginza, luxury hotels like the Mandarin Oriental and the Peninsula Tokyo offer world-class service. For a more budget-friendly option, consider staying in Asakusa, where you can find traditional ryokan (Japanese inns) offering tatami mat rooms and communal baths.

For a unique experience, consider a capsule hotel in Shinjuku or Shibuya, where you'll sleep in a compact pod but still have access to modern amenities. These are great for solo travelers or those who just need a place to crash for the night.

In Hakone, many inns offer onsen facilities, so you can soak in hot springs while enjoying mountain views. For a more rural experience, consider staying in Nikko, where many hotels blend traditional Japanese hospitality with modern comforts.

What NOT to Do in Tokyo and the Kanto Region

While Japan is an incredibly welcoming country, there are certain cultural norms and practices that travelers should be aware of. Do not speak loudly on public transport, as this is considered disrespectful to others. It's also important not to talk on your phone while on trains or buses—texting is fine, but phone conversations are a big no-no.

When visiting temples and shrines, always follow the proper etiquette. This includes bowing before entering, cleansing your hands at the chozuya (water basin), and not taking photos in areas where it's prohibited.

In restaurants, it's important not to leave a tip, as this can be seen as rude. The service charge is usually included, and tipping is not a common practice in Japan.

Finally, when visiting natural sites like Mount Fuji or Nikko, take care not to litter or disturb the environment. Japan places a high value on cleanliness, and travelers should respect this by disposing of trash properly and keeping public spaces clean.

• MOUNT FUJI AND CHUBU REGION

The Chubu region is often overlooked by travelers rushing between Tokyo and Kyoto, but for those who take the time to explore, it offers some of the most breathtaking landscapes and unique cultural experiences in Japan. Situated between Kanto and Kansai, Chubu stretches from the towering peaks of the Japanese Alps to the serene coastline of the Sea of Japan. The region includes nine prefectures: Niigata, Toyama, Ishikawa, Fukui, Yamanashi, Nagano, Gifu, Shizuoka, and Aichi.

At the heart of Chubu is Mount Fuji, Japan's highest and most iconic peak. This sacred mountain is more than just a postcard image; it's a spiritual symbol that has inspired poets, artists, and travelers for centuries. Beyond Mount Fuji, Chubu offers traditional villages like Shirakawa-go, modern cities such as Nagoya, and

162

stunning natural beauty in the form of hot springs, ski resorts, and national parks.

What to Do in the Chubu Region

For outdoor enthusiasts, Chubu is a paradise. A hike up Mount Fuji is a bucket-list item for many travelers. The climbing season typically runs from early July to mid-September, and there are several trails to choose from, depending on your fitness level and experience. The Yoshida Trail, starting from the Fifth Station, is the most popular and well-maintained, offering mountain huts where climbers can rest overnight. If you're not up for the hike, you can still enjoy stunning views of Mount Fuji from Lake Kawaguchi, one of the five lakes surrounding the mountain, where the reflection of Fuji in the water is simply magical, especially at dawn or dusk.

For a more relaxed experience, visit Hakone, located on the southeastern side of Chubu. It's famous for its hot springs (onsen) and spectacular views of Mount Fuji. Spend a day cruising on Lake Ashi, then take a cable car up to Owakudani, a volcanic valley known for its sulfurous hot springs. The black eggs boiled in the sulfuric waters are a local delicacy—legend has it that eating one will add seven years to your life!

If you're visiting in the winter, the Japanese Alps in Nagano offer some of the best skiing and snowboarding in Japan. Resorts like Hakuba and Nozawa Onsen attract powder enthusiasts from all over the world. Even if you don't ski, these resorts have great options for snowshoeing or soaking in outdoor hot springs while surrounded by snow-covered landscapes.

For those seeking history and culture, Takayama, in Gifu Prefecture, is a must-visit. This well-preserved Edo-period town offers traditional wooden houses, sake breweries, and lively morning markets. The Hida Folk Village just outside of Takayama is an open-air museum showcasing traditional thatched-roof houses from the region.

What Events to Enjoy in the Chubu Region

The Chubu region hosts a variety of traditional festivals throughout the year. One of the most famous is the Takayama Matsuri, held in spring and autumn in Takayama. It's one of Japan's top three festivals, featuring elaborate floats that parade through the town and beautifully costumed participants. The festival is a vibrant showcase of local craftsmanship and tradition, and at night, the floats are lit up, creating a magical atmosphere.

In Nagano, the Zenkoji Lantern Festival, held in February, is a captivating winter event. The streets leading to Zenkoji Temple are lined with thousands of paper lanterns, and the temple itself is bathed in a warm, glowing light, creating an ethereal scene.

For those visiting in autumn, the Koyo (autumn leaves) season in Chubu is spectacular. Korankei Gorge, near Nagoya, is famous for its maple trees that turn vibrant shades of red, orange, and yellow in late November. Walking through the gorge feels like stepping into a painting, especially during the evening when the trees are illuminated.

Where to Eat in the Chubu Region

The Chubu region offers a rich variety of local cuisine. In Nagoya, try the city's famous hitsumabushi, a grilled eel dish served over rice. The unique way of eating this dish allows you to enjoy it in different stages: first, savor the eel on its own, then mix it with condiments like green onions and wasabi, and finally, pour green tea or broth over the rice to create a comforting finish.

In Takayama, don't miss the local specialty, Hida beef, which is known for its marbled texture and rich flavor. You can enjoy it in various forms, from grilled steaks to Hida beef sushi served at local markets.

If you're in Shizuoka, wasabi is a regional delicacy, and many restaurants offer dishes incorporating this fresh and pungent ingredient. Visit a wasabi farm, like the Daio Wasabi Farm, where you can taste wasabi ice cream or wasabi-flavored noodles.

What to Eat in the Chubu Region

Chubu's local dishes are as varied as its landscapes. The region is famous for soba (buckwheat noodles), especially in Nagano, where the cold climate is ideal for growing high-quality buckwheat. Try Shinshu soba, known for its firm texture and earthy flavor, best enjoyed with a dipping sauce or in a hot broth.

In Toyama, seafood lovers should try Masu no sushi, a pressed sushi made with trout and wrapped in bamboo leaves, a delicacy that dates back to the Edo period. Another Toyama specialty is

Shiroebi (white shrimp), often served raw as sashimi or deep-fried as tempura.

If you find yourself in Ishikawa, the local Kaga kaiseki is a must. This traditional multi-course meal showcases seasonal ingredients from the sea and mountains, offering a refined and artful dining experience.

Where to Stay in the Chubu Region

The Chubu region offers a range of accommodations to suit every traveler's taste. For a traditional Japanese experience, stay in a ryokan with an onsen. Gero Onsen, located in Gifu, is one of Japan's top three hot spring areas, and many of the ryokan here offer luxurious baths with views of the surrounding mountains.

In Takayama, the Honjin Hiranoya Kachoan is a top-rated ryokan where you can enjoy traditional tatami rooms, multi-course meals, and private hot spring baths.

For those looking to stay near Mount Fuji, Kawaguchiko offers many lakeside hotels and guesthouses with spectacular views of the mountain. The Hoshinoya Fuji, a luxury glamping resort, provides modern cabins with large windows, allowing you to wake up to an unobstructed view of Fuji.

If you prefer a more modern stay, Nagoya has plenty of international hotel chains and boutique options in the city center, close to shopping, dining, and cultural sites.

What NOT to Do in the Chubu Region

When visiting the Chubu region, it's important to be mindful of local customs and practices. Do not underestimate the difficulty of climbing Mount Fuji—though it is popular, the ascent can be physically demanding, especially due to the altitude. If you decide to hike, bring proper gear, pace yourself, and stay hydrated.

Do not bathe in an onsen without first washing thoroughly. Onsen etiquette is very important in Japan, and cleanliness is a top priority. Be sure to rinse off completely before entering the communal bath.

Do not visit cultural or religious sites without respecting the proper decorum. For example, when visiting Shirakawa-go, be mindful that many of the thatched houses are private homes. Only enter those that are open to the public and avoid being disruptive to the residents.

Do not litter or leave your trash behind when visiting natural parks or hiking trails. Japan has a strong culture of cleanliness, and you are expected to carry your trash with you until you find a proper disposal bin.

Finally, do not expect to find English spoken widely, especially in rural areas. Learning a few basic Japanese phrases can go a long way in making your trip smoother and showing respect for the local culture.

• KYOTO AND KANSAI REGION

Kyoto, the ancient capital of Japan, is a city steeped in history and tradition. As the cultural heart of Japan, it's home to over 1,600 Buddhist temples, 400 Shinto shrines, and 17 UNESCO World Heritage Sites. For travelers seeking to immerse themselves in Japan's rich heritage, Kyoto is a must-visit destination.

The city is renowned for its serene gardens, elegant tea houses, and the graceful movements of geisha. With its blend of nature, history, and traditional Japanese arts, Kyoto offers a glimpse into the soul of the country.

Kyoto is divided into several distinct areas, each with its unique atmosphere. Higashiyama, on the eastern side, is famous for its preserved streets and historic temples like Kiyomizu-dera. The Arashiyama district, on the western outskirts of the city, is known for its scenic bamboo groves and the iconic Togetsukyo Bridge. In the north, you'll find the Golden Pavilion (Kinkaku-ji), while the central area is home to the Nijo Castle, a former residence of the shogun.

What to Do in Kyoto

Start your exploration of Kyoto with a visit to the Fushimi Inari Shrine, one of Japan's most iconic landmarks. Famous for its thousands of red torii gates that snake up Mount Inari, this Shinto shrine is dedicated to the gods of rice and agriculture. The hike to the summit takes about two to three hours, offering stunning views of the city along the way. It's best to visit early in the morning to avoid crowds.

Another must-see is Kiyomizu-dera, a Buddhist temple that offers panoramic views of Kyoto from its large wooden terrace. The temple is particularly beautiful during cherry blossom season in the spring and the vibrant autumn foliage in November. Nearby, the Ninenzaka and Sannenzaka streets are perfect for a leisurely stroll, where you can find traditional tea houses and souvenir shops.

For a more peaceful experience, visit Ryoan-ji, home to Japan's most famous Zen rock garden. The garden, with its 15 carefully arranged rocks, is designed to inspire contemplation and reflection. Ginkaku-ji (the Silver Pavilion) and its surrounding gardens are also worth a visit, especially for those interested in the Japanese aesthetic of wabi-sabi, which finds beauty in imperfection and impermanence.

Kyoto is also known for its tea culture, and a visit to the Uji district, located just outside the city, is highly recommended. Uji is famous for its high-quality green tea, and you can enjoy a traditional tea ceremony or sample matcha-flavored treats in one of the many tea shops.

What Events to Enjoy in Kyoto

Kyoto hosts numerous traditional festivals throughout the year, each offering a unique glimpse into Japan's cultural heritage. One of the most famous is the Gion Matsuri, held in July. This month-long festival is centered around the Gion district and features elaborate processions of large, ornate floats through the streets. The festival dates back over a thousand years and is considered one of Japan's most important cultural events.

In early August, the Daimonji Bonfire Festival is held, where large fires are lit on the mountains surrounding Kyoto to guide the spirits of the deceased back to the afterlife. The sight of the kanji characters glowing in the night sky is both solemn and awe-inspiring.

If you're visiting Kyoto in spring, don't miss the Miyako Odori, an annual geisha performance that showcases traditional Japanese dance and music. Held in the Gion district, this elegant event allows visitors to witness the beauty and grace of Kyoto's maiko and geiko (apprentice and fully-fledged geisha).

Discovering the Kansai Region

Beyond Kyoto, the Kansai region offers a diverse array of attractions, from modern cities to ancient temples. Kansai includes several major cities such as Osaka, Nara, Kobe, and Himeji, each offering its own unique experiences. Known as the cultural and historical cradle of Japan, Kansai is where tradition meets modernity.

Osaka, Japan's third-largest city, is a hub of culinary delights, nightlife, and entertainment. Often referred to as "Japan's kitchen," Osaka is famous for its street food, including takoyaki (octopus balls) and okonomiyaki (savory pancakes). Visit Dotonbori, the city's entertainment district, where neon lights reflect on the canal and food stalls line the streets.

Nara, just a short train ride from Kyoto, is another must-visit. As Japan's first permanent capital, Nara is home to the Todaiji Temple, which houses the world's largest bronze Buddha statue. In Nara Park, friendly deer roam freely, and visitors can feed them with special deer crackers sold by local vendors.

Himeji, located west of Kobe, is home to Himeji Castle, one of the most beautiful and best-preserved castles in Japan. Known as the White Heron Castle due to its pristine white exterior, it's a UNESCO World Heritage Site and an architectural masterpiece.

What to Do in the Kansai Region

In addition to the famous sites, Kansai is full of hidden gems. In Osaka, take a stroll through the Shinsekai district, an area that has retained its old-fashioned charm since the early 20th century. Visit the Tsutenkaku Tower for panoramic views of the city, and try local specialties like kushikatsu (deep-fried skewers) in one of the nearby restaurants.

For a more serene experience, explore Mount Koya (Koyasan) in Wakayama Prefecture, a sacred Buddhist temple complex that serves as the headquarters of the Shingon sect. Koyasan offers temple lodging (shukubo) where you can experience a monk's lifestyle, including vegetarian meals and early morning meditation sessions. Don't miss a visit to Okunoin Cemetery, the largest cemetery in Japan, where thousands of stone lanterns and moss-covered gravestones create an otherworldly atmosphere.

If you're looking for something off the beaten path, head to Amanohashidate in northern Kyoto Prefecture. This sandbar, known as one of Japan's "three scenic views," stretches across the bay, and visitors can enjoy a leisurely walk or bicycle ride while taking in the stunning coastal scenery.

Where to Eat in Kyoto and the Kansai Region

Kyoto is known for kaiseki, a traditional multi-course meal that highlights seasonal ingredients. For a truly authentic experience, try a kaiseki meal at a ryokan (traditional inn) or in one of the fine restaurants in the Pontocho or Gion districts. Some of Kyoto's most renowned kaiseki restaurants are located in these areas, where you can enjoy beautifully presented dishes in a refined, intimate setting.

If you're in the mood for something more casual, Kyoto is also famous for yudofu (tofu hot pot), which is a simple yet flavorful dish typically served in temple restaurants in Arashiyama.

Osaka, as mentioned earlier, is the place to indulge in street food. Head to Kuromon Ichiba Market, a bustling marketplace where you can sample fresh seafood, grilled meats, and Osaka's famous dishes. Another must-try is fugu (pufferfish), a delicacy served in specialized restaurants.

In Nara, try kakinoha-zushi, a type of sushi wrapped in persimmon leaves, a local specialty that dates back to the Edo period. The leaves impart a unique fragrance to the fish, which is typically mackerel or salmon.

What to Eat in Kyoto and the Kansai Region

In addition to kaiseki and yudofu, Kyoto is also famous for matcha (green tea) and matcha-based desserts. Visit Nishiki Market for a variety of matcha-flavored treats, including matcha ice cream, mochi, and cakes. The market is also a great place to try local pickles, dried fish, and fresh produce.

In Osaka, takoyaki and okonomiyaki are essential eats. These savory dishes can be found at street stalls and specialized

174

restaurants throughout the city. Osaka is also known for its love of ramen, and you'll find many ramen shops serving hearty bowls of noodles in rich, flavorful broths.

Where to Stay in Kyoto and the Kansai Region

Kyoto offers a range of accommodation options, from traditional ryokan to modern hotels. For a truly immersive experience, stay in a ryokan in the Higashiyama or Gion districts, where you can enjoy tatami rooms, futon bedding, and traditional Japanese meals. Some ryokan also offer private onsen baths with views of the surrounding gardens.

If you prefer modern comforts, Kyoto has many boutique hotels and international chains located near Kyoto Station. These are convenient for travelers who want easy access to public transportation and shopping areas.

In Osaka, the Umeda and Namba areas are popular places to stay. Umeda is more business-oriented, while Namba is known for its entertainment and dining options. If you're visiting Nara, consider staying in a ryokan near Nara Park, where you can wake up to the sight of deer grazing outside your window.

What NOT to Do in Kyoto and the Kansai Region

When visiting Kyoto and Kansai, it's important to respect local customs and traditions. Do not touch or feed the geisha or maiko in the Gion district. They are professional entertainers and should be treated with respect. If you wish to take photos, ask for permission first, and avoid obstructing their path.

Do not walk and eat at the same time, especially in more traditional areas like Kyoto. Eating while walking is considered rude in Japan. Instead, find a place to sit or stand while enjoying your food.

Do not speak loudly on public transportation, as quietness is highly valued in Japan. If you're traveling in a group, keep conversations low to avoid disturbing others.

Finally, do not litter. Japan is known for its cleanliness, and it's common for people to carry their trash with them until they find a proper disposal bin. Many areas, especially temples and parks, have limited trash cans, so plan accordingly.

● HIROSHIMA AND THE CHUGOKU REGION

Hiroshima is a city that holds immense historical significance, and for many travelers, visiting this city is both a journey through Japan's past and a reflection on the importance of peace. Devastated by the atomic bombing on August 6, 1945, Hiroshima has since transformed into a symbol of resilience and hope. Today, it is a thriving city that beautifully blends its tragic history with modern urban life and natural beauty.

The first stop for most visitors is the Hiroshima Peace Memorial Park, dedicated to the victims of the atomic bomb and the pursuit of world peace. The park is home to several poignant landmarks, including the Atomic Bomb Dome (Genbaku Dome), one of the few structures that survived the explosion. Nearby, you'll find the Hiroshima Peace Memorial Museum, which offers detailed exhibitions on the bombing, the aftermath, and Hiroshima's dedication to peace and nuclear disarmament. For a more serene and reflective experience, walk through the park's tree-lined paths and visit the Cenotaph and the Children's Peace Monument, where colorful paper cranes are left in tribute to Sadako Sasaki, a young victim of the bombing.

Beyond the Peace Park, Hiroshima offers a range of cultural and natural attractions. Shukkeien Garden, a beautifully landscaped

Japanese garden near Hiroshima Station, is a peaceful retreat from the bustling city. Modeled after the natural scenery of China, it features ponds, bridges, and tea houses. Stroll along the winding paths or stop at one of the pavilions for tea and a view of the garden's seasonal flowers.

A short ferry ride from Hiroshima takes you to Miyajima Island, famous for its floating Itsukushima Shrine. The shrine's torii gate, which appears to float on the water at high tide, is one of the most photographed sights in Japan. The island is also home to friendly deer, and visitors can hike up Mount Misen for panoramic views of the Seto Inland Sea.

What to Do in Hiroshima

When in Hiroshima, a visit to the Peace Memorial Park is essential, but there are many other experiences to enrich your trip. Begin your journey with a morning spent exploring the Hiroshima Castle, a reconstruction of the original structure destroyed in 1945. The castle grounds are home to beautiful cherry blossom trees in spring, and inside the castle, you'll find a museum dedicated to Hiroshima's history before the bombing.

Another fascinating attraction is the Hiroshima Orizuru Tower, where visitors can make and display their own paper cranes (orizuru) as symbols of peace. The rooftop observation deck offers a stunning view of the city and the Peace Memorial Park.

For a more immersive cultural experience, consider participating in a kagura performance, a traditional form of Shinto theatrical dance that tells stories of Japanese mythology. Many theaters in Hiroshima, such as Hiroshima Prefectural Art Museum, host kagura performances, and watching one is a unique way to connect with the region's cultural heritage.

For those seeking nature, a day trip to Sandankyo Gorge is highly recommended. Located about an hour and a half from Hiroshima, this hidden gem is a stunning ravine with crystal-clear waters, waterfalls, and lush forests. Hike the trails, take a boat ride, or simply relax and enjoy the beauty of the natural surroundings. It's an excellent escape from the city and relatively unknown to most tourists.

What not to do in and around Hiroshima

Traveling in Japan, particularly in a place with such a sensitive history as Hiroshima, comes with important cultural considerations. Here are a few key things to avoid:

Do not take photos in certain areas of the Peace Memorial Museum. While it's understandable to want to document your visit, there are parts of the museum, particularly those that display the personal belongings of atomic bomb victims, where photography is prohibited. Always be mindful of the signs and respectful of the somber nature of the exhibits.

Avoid loud conversations or disruptive behavior in quiet spaces. This applies particularly to places like Shukkeien Garden or the Peace Memorial Park, where a calm and reflective atmosphere is essential. Japanese culture values quiet and respect in public spaces, and this is even more crucial in memorial areas.

Do not litter. Japan is known for its cleanliness, and even though you may find it difficult to locate public trash bins, it's customary to hold onto your trash until you find an appropriate place to dispose of it.

Refrain from feeding the deer on Miyajima Island. While the deer may seem friendly and accustomed to human interaction, feeding them is discouraged as it can disrupt their natural diet and encourage bad behavior.

What Events to Enjoy in Hiroshima

Hiroshima hosts a variety of festivals and events throughout the year, providing unique opportunities to experience local culture and traditions. One of the most important is the Hiroshima Flower Festival, held annually in early May. The city transforms with colorful flower displays, parades, and performances, celebrating peace and resilience.

If you visit in August, the Peace Memorial Ceremony on August 6th is a solemn and significant event. Held at the Peace Memorial Park, this ceremony commemorates the atomic bombing and reaffirms Hiroshima's commitment to world peace. Thousands gather to offer prayers, make speeches, and float lanterns on the Motoyasu River.

For a more local experience, the Toka Ebisu Festival in January is a fun and lively event held at Hiroshima's Ebisu Shrine. This traditional festival, dedicated to the god of prosperity, features stalls selling good luck charms, food, and souvenirs, and is a great opportunity to experience local life.

Discovering the Chugoku Region

The Chugoku region, of which Hiroshima is a part, extends from the southern coast of Honshu to the Sea of Japan. While Hiroshima is the most well-known city, the region has much to offer, from ancient shrines to stunning coastlines. It's an area that is often overlooked by tourists, making it perfect for travelers seeking quieter, off-the-beaten-path experiences.

Okayama, located to the east of Hiroshima, is known for Korakuen Garden, one of Japan's three most famous landscape gardens. With its expansive lawns, ponds, and tea houses, it's a perfect place for a relaxing afternoon. Next to the garden is Okayama Castle, also known as "Crow Castle" due to its black exterior.

For a more spiritual experience, head to Izumo Taisha in Shimane Prefecture, one of Japan's oldest and most important Shinto shrines. Legend has it that the gods gather here once a year in October, making it a deeply spiritual place. The shrine's massive torii gate and ancient architecture are awe-inspiring.

What to Do in the Chugoku Region

A hidden gem in the Chugoku region is Tottori, famous for its dramatic sand dunes. The Tottori Sand Dunes stretch for miles along the coast, and visitors can enjoy activities like sandboarding or even a camel ride. The nearby Tottori Sand Museum features incredible sand sculptures from artists around the world.

If you're a fan of hiking, explore Mount Daisen in Tottori Prefecture, one of Japan's most beautiful and sacred mountains. The trails offer stunning views of the Sea of Japan, and in the winter, Daisen transforms into a popular ski destination.

For those seeking a unique cultural experience, visit the Bizen Osafune Sword Museum in Okayama Prefecture, where you can learn about the ancient art of Japanese sword-making. The museum offers demonstrations of traditional techniques, and you can even try your hand at crafting a small blade.

Where to Eat in Hiroshima and the Chugoku Region

Hiroshima is famous for its regional specialty, Hiroshima-style okonomiyaki, a savory pancake layered with cabbage, noodles, and various toppings, including pork, seafood, and cheese. Unlike the Osaka version, where ingredients are mixed, Hiroshima's okonomiyaki is made in layers, giving it a distinct texture and flavor. You can find okonomiyaki restaurants all over the city, but Okonomimura, a multi-level building dedicated to this dish, is a must-visit.

In Shimane, try Izumo soba, a type of buckwheat noodle that is served in small bowls with various toppings and sauces. It's a local delicacy and can be found at many traditional restaurants near Izumo Taisha.

What to Eat in Hiroshima and the Chugoku Region

Aside from okonomiyaki, Hiroshima is also known for its fresh oysters, particularly in the colder months. The city's proximity to the Seto Inland Sea ensures that the seafood here is some of the best in Japan. Head to Ujina Port or Miyajima Island to enjoy oysters prepared in various ways, from grilled to fried or served raw with a squeeze of lemon.

In Tottori, don't miss the chance to try Matsuba crab, a winter delicacy that is highly prized for its sweet and tender meat. You can find it served in sushi, tempura, or hot pot dishes at local restaurants.

Where to Stay in Hiroshima and the Chugoku Region

Hiroshima offers a range of accommodation options, from budget hostels to luxury hotels. If you're looking for a more traditional experience, stay at a ryokan on Miyajima Island, where you can enjoy stunning views of the sea and the torii gate from your room. Many ryokan also offer traditional meals featuring local seafood.

For those traveling through the Chugoku region, Okayama is a convenient base with a variety of hotels, including modern business hotels near the station. If you're visiting Izumo Taisha, consider staying at a traditional inn in Matsue, a charming town known for its historic castle and canals.

What NOT to Do in Hiroshima and the Chugoku Region

When visiting Hiroshima and the Chugoku region, it's important to respect the local customs and sensitivities, particularly regarding the atomic bombing. Do not make light of the tragic history or speak disrespectfully about it. Hiroshima is a place of deep reflection, and visitors are expected to act accordingly.

In rural areas of the Chugoku region, do not expect everyone to speak English. While larger cities like Hiroshima and Okayama are tourist-friendly, smaller towns may have limited English signage or speakers. Learning a few basic Japanese phrases or using a translation app can go a long way in showing respect to the locals.

Finally, do not rush your visit to this region. The Chugoku area is full of hidden treasures, and it's worth taking the time to explore beyond the usual tourist spots to experience the true beauty and culture of the region.

• THE TOHOKU REGION

The Tohoku region, located in the northern part of Honshu, is one of Japan's most underrated gems. Known for its unspoiled nature, hot springs, rugged mountains, and rich cultural heritage, Tohoku offers a glimpse into traditional Japan far from the bustling cities. Despite its beauty, Tohoku remains relatively untouched by mass tourism, making it an ideal destination for those seeking authentic experiences.

Tohoku is divided into six prefectures: Aomori, Akita, Iwate, Yamagata, Miyagi, and Fukushima. Each of these areas offers unique landscapes and cultural landmarks. Tohoku is particularly famous for its vibrant seasonal scenery—from the cherry blossoms in spring to the colorful foliage in autumn and snow-covered mountains in winter.

One of the region's most iconic sites is Lake Towada, a stunning crater lake straddling the border between Aomori and Akita prefectures. The lake is especially breathtaking in autumn when the surrounding forests burst into a symphony of red and gold leaves. Nearby, the Oirase Stream offers a scenic walking trail along a clear, fast-flowing stream with waterfalls and lush greenery.

For history lovers, Hiraizumi in Iwate Prefecture is a must-visit. Once a cultural rival to Kyoto, Hiraizumi is home to Chuson-ji Temple, a UNESCO World Heritage site, and the dazzling Konjikido Hall, covered entirely in gold leaf. This ancient town holds deep significance in Japanese history and offers visitors a serene and reflective experience.

In Miyagi Prefecture, the city of Sendai serves as a gateway to the region. It is known for its green spaces and Zuihoden, the mausoleum of the famous warlord Date Masamune. Just outside the city, Matsushima Bay, with its 260 pine-covered islands, is one of Japan's three most scenic views.

For those who enjoy off-the-beaten-path adventures, Tono in Iwate Prefecture is famous for its rural landscapes and folklore. Known as the "city of legends," Tono offers visitors a look into Japan's mythological past, where you can visit old farmhouses, witness traditional festivals, and hear stories of supernatural beings like the kappa, a mischievous water sprite.

What to Do in the Tohoku Region

1. Explore the Hot Springs (Onsen):
Tohoku is home to some of Japan's best onsen (hot springs). Nyuto Onsen in Akita Prefecture is one of the most famous, a rustic collection of outdoor baths nestled in the mountains. The hot spring waters here are believed to have healing properties, and each of the inns in Nyuto Onsen offers a unique bathing experience.

In Yamagata Prefecture, head to Ginzan Onsen, a charming hot spring town that feels like stepping back in time. The wooden ryokan (traditional inns) lining the Ginzan River are particularly beautiful when lit up at night, especially in winter when snow blankets the town.

2. Visit the Temples and Shrines:

The region is dotted with ancient temples and shrines, such as the Yamadera Temple in Yamagata Prefecture. Perched on a mountainside, this temple complex offers breathtaking views after climbing the 1,000 stone steps to the top. It is especially popular in autumn, when the surrounding trees turn vibrant shades of red and orange.

Another spiritual destination is Osorezan, or Mount Osore, in Aomori Prefecture. Known as the "gateway to the underworld," Osorezan is a sacred place for Buddhists and is surrounded by stark volcanic landscapes and sulfuric hot springs. Despite its eerie atmosphere, the temple grounds and surrounding area are tranquil and offer a deep sense of spiritual reflection.

3. Hike and Enjoy the Outdoors:

Tohoku's natural beauty is perfect for outdoor activities, particularly hiking. Mount Bandai in Fukushima Prefecture is a dormant volcano that offers excellent hiking trails and panoramic views of the surrounding lakes and forests. In summer, the area around Urabandai transforms into a lush green paradise, while in winter, it becomes a popular ski destination.

The Dewa Sanzan in Yamagata Prefecture is another pilgrimage site, consisting of three sacred mountains: Haguro, Gassan, and Yudono. Pilgrims and hikers alike visit these mountains to walk the ancient trails, admire the towering cedar trees, and visit the temples and shrines that dot the landscape.

4. Take a Scenic Drive:

If you prefer to explore by car, the Bandai-Azuma Skyline in Fukushima offers one of the most scenic drives in Japan. This mountain road winds through the Azuma Mountains, offering breathtaking views of volcanic craters, rugged landscapes, and the surrounding valleys. In autumn, the road is particularly popular for its fall foliage.

What Events to Enjoy in the Tohoku Region

Tohoku is known for its vibrant festivals, many of which have centuries-old traditions.

1. Nebuta Matsuri (Aomori):
Held every August in Aomori City, the Nebuta Matsuri is one of Japan's most famous festivals. Giant, illuminated paper floats depicting gods, warriors, and mythical creatures are paraded through the streets to the beat of drums and flutes. The festival's energy is contagious, and visitors are welcome to join the procession.

2. Kanto Matsuri (Akita):
In Akita, the Kanto Matsuri is held in early August and is known for its impressive display of skill. Participants balance large bamboo poles (up to 12 meters tall) adorned with paper lanterns on their foreheads, shoulders, and hips. The sight of dozens of these poles swaying through the streets is a true spectacle.

3. Sendai Tanabata Festival (Miyagi):
Sendai's Tanabata Festival in August is another must-see event. The streets are adorned with colorful streamers and decorations, creating a festive atmosphere. The festival celebrates the star-

crossed lovers of Japanese mythology, and the city is filled with food stalls, performances, and traditional music.

Where to Eat in the Tohoku Region

Tohoku is known for its hearty and flavorful cuisine, much of which is influenced by the region's cold winters and agricultural traditions.

1. Wanko Soba (Iwate):

For a unique dining experience, try Wanko Soba in Iwate. This dish consists of small bowls of soba noodles served continuously until the diner is full—sometimes you might eat up to 100 bowls! It's a fun and interactive way to enjoy a local specialty.

2. Yonezawa Beef (Yamagata):

In Yamagata, don't miss the chance to try Yonezawa beef, one of Japan's top wagyu brands. Known for its tender texture and rich flavor, Yonezawa beef is served in a variety of dishes, including sukiyaki, steak, and shabu-shabu.

3. Kiritanpo (Akita):

Kiritanpo is a traditional dish from Akita made of mashed rice shaped around a skewer and grilled. It's often served in hot pots with chicken and vegetables. The comforting flavors make it a perfect dish for the region's colder months.

What to Eat in the Tohoku Region

Tohoku's agricultural bounty means that you'll find fresh, locally produced ingredients in most dishes. Here are some must-try regional specialties:

1. Apples (Aomori):
Aomori is famous for its apples, and no visit is complete without trying one. You'll find apple-flavored products everywhere, from cider to pies and even apple-infused curry.

2. Zunda (Miyagi):
Zunda is a sweet paste made from mashed edamame (soybeans), and it's a specialty of Miyagi. Zunda is often served on mochi (rice cakes) or as a topping for desserts like parfaits.

3. Anko Nabe (Fukushima):
Anko nabe is a hot pot dish made from anglerfish, a deep-sea fish known for its rich, gelatinous meat. It's a warming and flavorful dish that's especially popular in coastal areas of Fukushima.

Where to Stay in the Tohoku Region

Tohoku offers a wide range of accommodations, from luxury ryokan to budget-friendly inns and hotels.

1. Ryokan at Nyuto Onsen (Akita):
For an authentic onsen experience, stay at one of the ryokan in Nyuto Onsen. Many of these traditional inns offer outdoor baths

with views of the surrounding forest, providing a serene and relaxing atmosphere.

2. Boutique Hotels in Sendai (Miyagi):
In Sendai, there are several boutique hotels that blend modern amenities with traditional Japanese hospitality. Staying in the city offers easy access to the region's attractions and a variety of dining options.

3. Farm Stays (Iwate):
For a unique experience, consider a farm stay in Tono, where you can live with a local family, help with farm activities, and enjoy home-cooked meals made from fresh, local ingredients. It's an excellent way to experience rural life and the region's agricultural traditions.

What NOT to Do in the Tohoku Region

1. Don't Underestimate the Weather:
Tohoku's winters can be harsh, with heavy snowfalls and freezing temperatures, particularly in Aomori, Akita, and Iwate. Be sure to pack appropriate clothing if you're visiting during the colder months, and check the weather forecasts before heading out on outdoor adventures.

2. Don't Expect Fast Travel:
While Tohoku is connected by the Shinkansen (bullet train), many of its more rural areas require buses or local trains to reach. Travel times can be longer than expected, so plan your itinerary with some flexibility. Enjoy the slower pace, and don't rush through the region.

3. Don't Forget to Show Respect at Temples and Shrines:
As in other parts of Japan, visitors to Tohoku's temples and shrines should be mindful of etiquette. Bow at the entrance, refrain from taking photos in restricted areas, and always maintain a respectful attitude, particularly in sacred or historical sites like Osorezan or Yamadera.

• SAPPORO AND THE HOKKAIDO REGION

Hokkaido, the northernmost island of Japan, is a vast region known for its breathtaking natural beauty, distinct seasons, and rich cultural heritage. Unlike the bustling metropolises of Tokyo or

Osaka, Hokkaido offers wide open spaces, majestic mountains, pristine lakes, and rolling fields. Whether you're visiting in the depths of winter for the world-famous snow festivals or exploring its lush landscapes in the summer, Hokkaido promises unforgettable experiences.

Sapporo, the capital city of Hokkaido, serves as the gateway to the island. It's a vibrant city that blends modernity with nature, boasting wide streets, green parks, and a laid-back atmosphere. Famous for the annual Sapporo Snow Festival, the city is also home to historical sites, delicious food, and unique shopping experiences. Beyond Sapporo, the island is rich in destinations worth exploring.

Hokkaido is divided into several distinct areas, each offering unique attractions. To the east, you'll find the stunning Shiretoko Peninsula, a UNESCO World Heritage site where wildlife thrives and unspoiled nature reigns supreme. The central region is home to the Daisetsuzan National Park, known for its expansive wilderness and hiking trails. To the north, the Wakkanai area offers beautiful coastal scenery, while the southern region of Hakodate boasts one of Japan's most picturesque night views.

One of the major draws of Hokkaido is its four distinct seasons, each offering different experiences. Winter transforms the island into a wonderland of snow, perfect for skiing and snowboarding in resorts like Niseko and Furano. Spring and summer bring vibrant flowers, green fields, and outdoor activities like cycling and hiking.

Autumn offers a stunning display of fall foliage, particularly in places like Jozankei and Sounkyo.

What to Do in the Hokkaido Region

1. Explore Sapporo

Start your Hokkaido adventure in Sapporo, where you can stroll through Odori Park, a long, narrow green space in the heart of the city that transforms with each season. In winter, Odori Park hosts the Sapporo Snow Festival, showcasing massive snow sculptures. During warmer months, it's a relaxing spot to enjoy nature.

Visit the Sapporo Beer Museum, where you can learn about the history of Japan's oldest beer brand and even sample some local brews. For a taste of the city's history, head to Sapporo Clock Tower and Hokkaido Shrine—both important cultural landmarks.

2. Visit the Blue Pond in Biei

One of Hokkaido's hidden gems is the Blue Pond in Biei, a surreal and enchanting spot where the water's vibrant blue color changes depending on the light. The pond is set against a backdrop of mountains and trees, creating a picturesque scene that feels otherworldly. It's particularly striking in early morning or just after a rainfall.

3. Skiing and Snowboarding in Niseko and Furano

Hokkaido is world-famous for its powder snow, drawing winter sports enthusiasts from around the globe. Niseko, located near Mount Yotei, is one of Japan's premier ski destinations, offering a variety of slopes for all skill levels and an international atmosphere. If you prefer a quieter alternative, head to Furano, where you'll find excellent skiing without the large crowds.

4. Hiking in Daisetsuzan National Park

For outdoor enthusiasts, Daisetsuzan National Park is a paradise of rugged mountains, hot springs, and hiking trails. The park is Hokkaido's largest, covering 2,267 square kilometers, and is home to some of Japan's most pristine wilderness.

Popular hikes include climbing Mount Asahi (Asahidake), Hokkaido's highest peak, or trekking through the Sounkyo Gorge, where you'll encounter waterfalls, stunning rock formations, and vibrant autumn colors.

5. Wildlife Watching on the Shiretoko Peninsula

The Shiretoko Peninsula is one of Japan's most remote and wild areas, making it a haven for wildlife lovers. This UNESCO World Heritage site is home to brown bears, foxes, deer, and a variety of bird species.

Take a boat tour along the coast to see the rugged cliffs and possibly spot whales or dolphins. If you're visiting in winter, try the drift ice walking experience, where you can walk on the frozen sea off the coast of Shiretoko.

What Events to Enjoy in the Hokkaido Region

1. Sapporo Snow Festival

The Sapporo Snow Festival, held every February, is Hokkaido's most famous event. Thousands of people from around the world gather to see the giant, intricate snow and ice sculptures that line Odori Park. The festival features food stalls, live music, and even a snow slide for children. It's a magical time to visit Sapporo, with the entire city transformed into a winter wonderland.

2. Yosakoi Soran Festival (Sapporo)

If you're visiting in June, don't miss the Yosakoi Soran Festival, a vibrant celebration of traditional and modern dance. Thousands of performers from all over Japan gather in Sapporo to perform energetic, choreographed dances to the rhythm of traditional folk music. The festival brings the streets of Sapporo alive with color, music, and dance.

3. Lavender Festival (Furano)

In July, Furano's Lavender Festival celebrates the peak bloom of the region's famous lavender fields. Farm Tomita is the most popular spot to see the vibrant purple fields stretching as far as the eye can see. The festival includes lavender-scented products, food stalls selling lavender ice cream, and live performances.

Where to Eat in the Hokkaido Region

Hokkaido is known for its fresh seafood, dairy products, and agricultural bounty, making it a food lover's paradise.

1. Seafood in Hakodate

Head to Hakodate Asaichi (Morning Market) to sample some of the freshest seafood Hokkaido has to offer. Try a bowl of kaisendon, a rice bowl topped with fresh sashimi such as salmon, uni (sea urchin), and ikura (salmon roe). Don't miss the local specialty, squid, which is served fresh or grilled.

2. Ramen in Sapporo

Hokkaido is the birthplace of miso ramen, and there's no better place to try it than in Sapporo. Visit Ganso Sapporo Ramen Yokocho, a narrow alley filled with tiny ramen shops, each offering its own take on the famous dish.

The rich, miso-based broth, combined with thick noodles and toppings like butter, corn, and pork, makes for a hearty meal perfect for Hokkaido's chilly weather.

3. Dairy in Furano

Furano is known for its high-quality dairy products, thanks to the region's lush pastures and clean air. Stop by Furano Cheese Factory to sample fresh cheeses, yogurt, and milk-based sweets. You can also try your hand at making your own butter or ice cream.

What to Eat in the Hokkaido Region

1. Jingisukan (Grilled Lamb)

One of Hokkaido's most iconic dishes is jingisukan, a grilled lamb dish named after the Mongolian warrior Genghis Khan. The meat is grilled on a special dome-shaped grill and is served with vegetables like onions and bean sprouts. You can find this dish at many restaurants in Sapporo and across Hokkaido.

2. Kaisen-don (Seafood Rice Bowl)

As mentioned, Hokkaido is famous for its fresh seafood, and one of the best ways to enjoy it is in a kaisen-don. This dish features a bed of rice topped with an assortment of fresh sashimi, including salmon, tuna, shrimp, and sea urchin. You can find kaisen-don in many markets across the island, but the best places to try it are in Hakodate or Otaru.

3. Soft Cream

Hokkaido's dairy industry is renowned, and you can't leave without trying soft cream, the local version of soft-serve ice cream. Hokkaido soft cream is richer and creamier than what you might find elsewhere in Japan. Look for seasonal flavors like lavender (in Furano) or melon, which are unique to the region.

Where to Stay in the Hokkaido Region

1. Ryokan in Jozankei Onsen (Sapporo)

For a relaxing stay, book a night at a ryokan in Jozankei Onsen, located just outside Sapporo. This hot spring town is nestled in a valley surrounded by mountains, and many ryokan offer rooms with private onsen baths. It's a perfect escape from the city and a chance to unwind in the natural hot spring waters.

2. Boutique Hotels in Furano

Furano offers a range of accommodations, from budget-friendly hostels to luxury hotels. For a unique stay, consider booking a room at one of Furano's boutique hotels, where you can enjoy stunning views of the surrounding countryside and access to the famous lavender fields.

3. Luxury Ski Resorts in Niseko

If you're visiting Niseko for skiing, stay at one of the luxury ski resorts that offer slope-side accommodations, gourmet dining, and onsen facilities. Many resorts in Niseko cater to international guests and offer English-speaking staff, making it a convenient choice for non-Japanese speakers.

What NOT to Do in the Hokkaido Region

1. Don't Underestimate the Weather:

Hokkaido's winters are known for being harsh, with heavy snowfall and freezing temperatures. If you're visiting in winter, be sure to dress in layers and bring appropriate gear for the cold. The roads can be icy, so if you're driving, make sure to rent a car equipped with snow tires.

2. Don't Forget to Respect Nature:
Hokkaido's wilderness is one of its biggest attractions, but it's important to respect the natural environment. When hiking, stay on marked trails and don't leave litter behind. In areas like Shiretoko, where wildlife like bears roam, follow local guidelines to avoid disturbing the animals.

3. Don't Rush Through Hokkaido:
Hokkaido is a large island with much to explore, and it's tempting to try and see everything in one trip. However, it's best to take your time and truly enjoy the region's natural beauty.

• THE SHIKOKU REGION

Shikoku, the smallest of Japan's four main islands, offers a deeply immersive experience in traditional Japanese culture, stunning natural beauty, and a slower, more laid-back pace compared to its larger counterparts. Shikoku is famous for its pilgrimage route dedicated to Kobo Daishi, one of Japan's most revered Buddhist monks. This route, known as the 88 Temple Pilgrimage, takes travelers around the island to visit 88 sacred temples. It's a journey that offers spiritual enlightenment as well as breathtaking landscapes.

Shikoku is divided into four prefectures: Ehime, Kagawa, Tokushima, and Kochi. Each of these regions has its unique attractions and history. From the Uchiko's traditional towns and historical preservation areas in Ehime to the Iya Valley in Tokushima with its hidden vine bridges and lush forests, Shikoku promises a wealth of experiences for every type of traveler.

Though often overlooked by international tourists, Shikoku provides a perfect blend of authentic Japanese experiences, stunning rural landscapes, and coastal beauty. You can explore the bustling castle towns, soak in hot springs, hike through ancient forests, or taste some of Japan's finest udon noodles. Shikoku is also famous for its rivers and valleys, such as the Shimanto River and Oboke Gorge, both offering opportunities for scenic boat rides and adventurous rafting.

What to Do in the Shikoku Region

1. Visit Matsuyama Castle (Ehime)
Matsuyama Castle is one of Japan's best-preserved original castles and is located in the city of Matsuyama, Ehime Prefecture. Perched atop Mount Katsuyama, it offers panoramic views of the city and the Seto Inland Sea.

To reach the castle, you can either hike through a beautiful park or take a ropeway, making the journey a scenic and enjoyable experience. The castle grounds are particularly beautiful during the cherry blossom season.

2. Explore the Iya Valley (Tokushima)

One of Shikoku's most dramatic landscapes, the Iya Valley is a remote and stunning area known for its steep gorges, vine bridges, and untouched nature. The Kazurabashi Vine Bridge is a must-see, suspended over the emerald waters of the Iya River. Originally built from vines by locals, the bridge has been reconstructed but still retains its rustic charm. The valley is also an ideal destination for hiking, with trails leading to secluded villages and waterfalls. Iya is one of Shikoku's best-kept secrets, offering a peaceful escape into nature.

3. The 88 Temple Pilgrimage

The 88 Temple Pilgrimage is one of Shikoku's defining experiences. Though completing all 88 temples can take weeks on foot, many travelers choose to visit a select few to gain insight into the region's deep religious significance. Some of the most important temples include Ryozenji, the first temple on the pilgrimage, and Zentsuji Temple, the birthplace of Kobo Daishi. Whether you're a pilgrim or a curious traveler, visiting these temples offers a glimpse into Japan's spiritual side, and the surrounding landscapes make the journey just as rewarding.

4. Naoshima Island (Kagawa)

Although technically part of the Seto Inland Sea, Naoshima Island is easily accessible from Shikoku and is renowned for its modern art installations. The island is home to the famous Chichu Art Museum and Benesse House, where contemporary artworks are integrated into the island's landscape. A day trip to Naoshima provides a unique blend of nature and art, making it a must-visit for art enthusiasts.

5. Ritsurin Garden (Takamatsu, Kagawa)

Ritsurin Garden in Takamatsu is one of Japan's most beautiful traditional landscape gardens. Spanning over 400 years of history, this garden features ponds, meticulously pruned pine trees, and a backdrop of Mount Shiun. Visitors can take a boat ride on the central pond, enjoy a traditional tea ceremony in the tea house, or simply stroll through the garden's various scenic paths. Ritsurin Garden is a perfect example of Japanese landscape design and offers a serene escape from the city.

What Events to Enjoy in the Shikoku Region

1. Awa Odori (Tokushima)

Held annually in August, Awa Odori is one of Japan's most famous dance festivals, attracting thousands of visitors from all over the country. The streets of Tokushima come alive with lively traditional dance performances accompanied by taiko drums, shamisen, and flutes. Participants wear colorful yukata (summer kimono) and dance in synchronized movements, creating an energetic and joyful atmosphere. If you're visiting Shikoku in summer, experiencing Awa Odori is a must.

2. Yosakoi Matsuri (Kochi)

Yosakoi Matsuri in Kochi is another vibrant summer festival that blends traditional and modern dance styles. Held in August, this festival features colorful costumes, dynamic performances, and powerful music. The participants dance in teams, often incorporating unique elements into their performances, such as naruko (wooden clappers). The streets of Kochi come alive with the energy and creativity of this spectacular event.

3. Uwajima Bullfighting (Ehime)

A unique cultural event in Ehime Prefecture is Uwajima Bullfighting, which takes place multiple times a year in Uwajima City. Unlike Spanish bullfighting, this event involves two bulls competing against each other in a test of strength, without any harm to the animals. The bulls are trained athletes, and the competition is more about the bulls' skill and power. It's a fascinating and lesser-known cultural experience that offers a glimpse into the local traditions of Shikoku.

Where to Eat in the Shikoku Region

Shikoku is renowned for its simple yet delicious cuisine, influenced by the island's natural resources, agricultural products, and seafood.

1. Udon Noodles in Kagawa

Kagawa Prefecture is often called the "Udon Prefecture" because of its famous Sanuki Udon. These thick, chewy noodles are typically served in a light broth or cold with a dipping sauce. For a truly authentic experience, visit one of the many local udon shops where you can watch the noodles being made fresh and choose from a variety of toppings. A popular spot is Yamada Udon in Takamatsu, where you can sample different types of udon at an affordable price.

2. Jakoten in Ehime

Jakoten is a local specialty in Ehime, made from ground fish that's deep-fried into a savory fish cake. It's a popular snack and can be found at food stalls or served as part of a meal. Pair it with a glass of local sake for a true taste of Shikoku.

3. Bonito Tataki in Kochi

Kochi Prefecture is famous for its bonito tataki, a dish of lightly seared bonito (skipjack tuna) served with garlic, ginger, and ponzu sauce. The fish is seared over a straw fire, giving it a unique smoky flavor. Hirome Market in Kochi City is an excellent place to try this dish, as it offers a lively atmosphere with numerous stalls serving fresh seafood.

What to Eat in the Shikoku Region

1. Soba (Buckwheat Noodles)

Shikoku is home to high-quality soba, particularly in the mountainous regions of Tokushima and Kochi. The fresh, earthy flavor of the buckwheat noodles is best enjoyed in a simple broth or served cold with a dipping sauce.

2. Citrus Fruits

Shikoku is famous for its citrus fruits, particularly mikan (mandarin oranges) from Ehime Prefecture. The region's mild climate and fertile soil produce some of Japan's sweetest and juiciest citrus fruits. You'll find mikan in a variety of forms, from fresh fruit to juice and sweets.

3. Salted Sea Bream (Tai no Shioyaki)

In coastal areas, particularly around Naruto, you can try tai no shioyaki (grilled sea bream). The fish is salted and grilled over an open flame, offering a simple yet delicious flavor that highlights the freshness of the seafood.

Where to Stay in the Shikoku Region

1. Dogo Onsen (Matsuyama, Ehime)

For a traditional Japanese experience, stay at an onsen ryokan in Dogo Onsen, one of Japan's oldest and most famous hot spring resorts. The main attraction is the Dogo Onsen Honkan, a historical bathhouse that inspired Studio Ghibli's "Spirited Away." Many of the nearby ryokan offer private baths, traditional meals, and a chance to relax in a serene atmosphere.

2. Guesthouses in Iya Valley

For those seeking a more rustic and off-the-beaten-path experience, consider staying in a guesthouse in the Iya Valley. These family-run accommodations offer a chance to experience traditional Japanese rural life, often with home-cooked meals made from local ingredients. Staying in the valley also allows you to explore the area's natural beauty at your own pace.

3. Boutique Hotels in Takamatsu

If you prefer modern comforts, Takamatsu offers a range of boutique hotels that cater to international travelers. These hotels provide easy access to the city's attractions, including Ritsurin

Garden and the ferry terminal for day trips to the Seto Inland Sea islands.

What NOT to Do in the Shikoku Region

1. Don't Skip the Smaller Towns and Villages
Many travelers focus only on the main cities like Matsuyama and Takamatsu, but Shikoku's smaller towns and rural areas hold much of the island's charm. Villages like Uchiko and Ozu offer a glimpse into traditional life with beautifully preserved architecture and tranquil streets.

2. Don't Disrespect Local Customs at Temples
If you choose to visit any of the 88 pilgrimage temples, remember to respect the local customs. When entering a temple, be sure to cleanse your hands and mouth at the water basin, bow before entering, and refrain from loud talking or inappropriate behavior.

3. Don't Rush Through Your Journey
Shikoku is an island that encourages slow travel. Rather than trying to see everything quickly, take the time to explore each region deeply. Enjoy the landscapes, meet the locals, and savor the simple beauty of rural Japan.

• THE KYUSHU AND OKINAWA REGION

Kyushu, the southernmost of Japan's four main islands, is a region known for its diverse landscapes, rich history, and vibrant culture. From active volcanoes and lush national parks to historical sites and hot springs, Kyushu has something for every type of traveler. Meanwhile, Okinawa, located southwest of Kyushu, is known for its stunning beaches, tropical climate, and unique blend of Japanese and indigenous Ryukyu culture.

Kyushu boasts some of Japan's most famous volcanoes, including Mount Aso, one of the world's largest active volcanic calderas. It is also home to the historic city of Kumamoto, with its majestic castle, and Nagasaki, which has a rich history as a former port for international trade. Okinawa, on the other hand, is famous for its beautiful coral reefs, making it a paradise for snorkeling and diving enthusiasts. Together, these regions offer a blend of adventure, relaxation, and cultural exploration.

What to Do in the Kyushu and Okinawa Region

1. Visit Kumamoto Castle (Kumamoto Prefecture)

Kumamoto Castle is one of Japan's most impressive castles, renowned for its unique architectural style and striking black exterior. The castle was built in the 17th century and is surrounded by beautiful gardens and impressive stone walls. Although it suffered damage during the 2016 earthquake, restoration efforts are ongoing, and parts of the castle are still accessible. Be sure to explore the surrounding Suizenji Jojuen Garden, which beautifully represents the landscape of Japan.

2. Explore Mount Aso (Kumamoto Prefecture)

Mount Aso is an active volcano and one of Japan's most iconic natural landmarks. Visitors can hike to the crater, explore the surrounding lush grasslands, and enjoy panoramic views of the caldera. For those less inclined to hike, consider taking a scenic drive around the caldera, stopping at Kusasenrigahama, a grassy plain that offers stunning views and a perfect picnic spot. Don't forget to visit one of the local onsen (hot springs) to relax after your adventures.

3. Discover Nagasaki's History

Nagasaki is steeped in history and was a significant port city during Japan's period of isolation. The Nagasaki Peace Park and the Atomic Bomb Museum provide a poignant reminder of the events of World War II and their impact on the city. Visitors can also explore the historic Dejima, an island that served as the only place for foreign trade during Japan's isolation. The charming streets of Glover Garden and Oura Church showcase the unique blend of Western and Japanese architecture.

4. Relax at Beppu's Hot Springs (Oita Prefecture)

Beppu is famous for its many hot springs, known as onsen, and is often referred to as the "onsen capital" of Japan. Visitors can enjoy unique hot spring experiences, such as the Hells of Beppu, which are colorful hot springs that are not meant for bathing but are fascinating to see. For a relaxing soak, try one of the many ryokan (traditional inns) or public baths, where you can enjoy the therapeutic waters.

5. Beach Hopping in Okinawa

Okinawa is famous for its pristine beaches and turquoise waters. Naha, the capital city, is a great starting point for exploring the nearby beaches. Kokusai Dori (International Road) is lined with shops and restaurants, and from there, you can easily reach the beautiful Naminoue Beach. For a more secluded experience, consider visiting Zamami Island, known for its stunning beaches and snorkeling opportunities. The islands of Kerama are a short ferry ride away from Naha and offer breathtaking coral reefs and vibrant marine life.

6. Discover the Ryukyu Culture in Okinawa

Okinawa has a unique cultural heritage distinct from mainland Japan, influenced by its historical Ryukyu Kingdom. Visitors should explore the Shurijo Castle, a UNESCO World Heritage site that reflects the island's royal history. Participate in traditional Ryukyu dance performances and try local crafts, such as bingata (stencil-dyed textiles). Don't miss the chance to taste Okinawa soba, a local noodle dish that differs from its mainland counterpart.

What Events to Enjoy in the Kyushu and Okinawa Region

1. Nagasaki Kunchi Festival

The Nagasaki Kunchi Festival is held annually in October and is one of Japan's most vibrant festivals. It celebrates the city's diverse cultural influences and features colorful floats, traditional dances, and performances that showcase Nagasaki's unique blend of cultures.

The festival highlights the history of the city, dating back to the days of international trade, and culminates in a grand parade.

2. Kumamoto Castle's Cherry Blossom Festival

Every spring, Kumamoto Castle hosts a stunning cherry blossom festival that draws thousands of visitors. The castle grounds are adorned with over 800 cherry trees, creating a picturesque scene that is perfect for hanami (flower viewing). This event offers food stalls, traditional performances, and a chance to enjoy the beauty of the sakura in the historic setting of the castle.

3. Okinawa Zento Matsuri

Held in October, the Okinawa Zento Matsuri is a celebration of Okinawan culture, featuring traditional music, dance, and food. The streets of Naha come alive with parades and performances that showcase the island's unique heritage. Visitors can enjoy local delicacies, participate in cultural workshops, and immerse themselves in the lively atmosphere.

Where to Eat in the Kyushu and Okinawa Region

1. Hakata Ramen (Fukuoka)

Fukuoka, the capital of Kyushu, is famous for its rich and flavorful Hakata ramen. The thin, straight noodles are served in a creamy tonkotsu (pork bone) broth and topped with chashu (braised pork), green onions, and nori (seaweed). Visit the bustling Yatai food stalls along the riverside for an authentic dining experience.

2. Goya Champuru (Okinawa)

In Okinawa, try goya champuru, a traditional stir-fry dish made with bitter melon (goya), tofu, pork, and various vegetables. The dish is both nutritious and delicious, offering a taste of Okinawan cuisine that reflects the local emphasis on health.

3. Chicken Nanban (Kagoshima)

Chicken nanban is a popular dish in Kagoshima Prefecture, featuring fried chicken marinated in a tangy vinegar sauce and served with tartar sauce. The combination of crispy chicken and flavorful sauce makes it a must-try for food lovers.

What to Eat in the Kyushu and Okinawa Region

1. Sata Andagi (Okinawa)

Sata andagi are traditional Okinawan doughnuts, crispy on the outside and soft on the inside. They are often served at festivals and make for a delightful snack. Look for stalls selling these treats at local markets or festivals.

2. Tonkotsu Ramen (Fukuoka)

Fukuoka's tonkotsu ramen is a signature dish that every visitor should try. The broth, made by boiling pork bones for hours, has a rich flavor that is often enhanced with garlic, green onions, and slices of chashu. Pair it with a side of gyoza (dumplings) for a complete meal.

3. Shirobuta (Kumamoto)

Kumamoto is known for its high-quality pork, especially the shirobuta (white pig). Enjoy this tender and flavorful meat grilled or as part of a hot pot dish. Many restaurants in Kumamoto specialize in shirobuta, providing a delicious experience for meat lovers.

Where to Stay in the Kyushu and Okinawa Region

1. Ryokan in Beppu

Experience traditional Japanese hospitality by staying in a ryokan in Beppu. Many ryokan offer onsen facilities, allowing guests to relax in the soothing hot springs. Some popular choices include Yufuin Onsen and Hoshino Resorts KAI Beppu, where you can enjoy kaiseki (multi-course) meals and stunning views.

2. Luxury Hotels in Fukuoka

Fukuoka boasts a range of luxury hotels, such as The Grand Hyatt Fukuoka and Hotel Nikko Fukuoka, which offer modern amenities and convenient access to the city's attractions. Enjoy comfortable accommodations and a variety of dining options during your stay.

3. Beach Resorts in Okinawa

Okinawa is home to several beautiful beach resorts, including The Busena Terrace and ANA InterContinental Manza Beach Resort. These resorts offer stunning ocean views, direct beach access, and various activities, making them ideal for a relaxing getaway.

What NOT to Do in the Kyushu and Okinawa Region

1. Don't Disregard Local Customs

When visiting temples and shrines, be respectful of local customs. This includes bowing when entering, cleansing your hands at purification fountains, and refraining from loud behavior. Understanding and respecting local traditions will enhance your experience and show appreciation for the culture.

2. Don't Limit Yourself to Tourist Spots

While popular attractions are worth visiting, don't miss out on the hidden gems scattered throughout Kyushu and Okinawa. Explore smaller towns, local markets, and off-the-beaten-path destinations to gain a deeper understanding of the region's culture and lifestyle.

3. Don't Rush Your Experience

Traveling in Kyushu and Okinawa is best done at a leisurely pace. Take the time to savor the local cuisine, engage with locals, and immerse yourself in the natural beauty of the region. Avoid cramming too many activities into one day; instead, focus on quality experiences.

4. Don't Forget Sunscreen in Okinawa

With its tropical climate and beautiful beaches, don't forget to apply sunscreen and stay hydrated while exploring Okinawa. Protecting your skin from the sun will ensure you enjoy your time without discomfort.

From our perspective and experience, the Kyushu and Okinawa region offers a captivating blend of history, culture, and natural beauty. From the majestic landscapes of Mount Aso to the vibrant coral reefs of Okinawa, this area of Japan has something to offer every traveler. By respecting local customs, exploring hidden gems, and savoring unique cuisine, visitors can create unforgettable memories in this diverse and welcoming region. Enjoy your journey through Kyushu and Okinawa, where every moment is an opportunity for discovery!

CONCLUSION

As we draw this journey to a close, it's essential to remember that Japan is a land of contrast and harmony, where ancient traditions coexist with cutting-edge innovation. Whether you've marveled at the bustling streets of Tokyo, wandered through the serene temples of Kyoto, or discovered the culinary delights of Osaka, each experience has been a chapter in your own story of exploration.

Travel, at its heart, is about connection. It's about bridging gaps between diverse cultures and finding common ground. In Japan, this connection is palpable in the warm hospitality of the people, the meticulous care in every detail, and the profound respect for nature and history. As you navigate through this fascinating country, remember to embrace these connections, allowing them to enrich your journey and broaden your perspective.

For those moments when the language barrier feels daunting, take solace in the universal language of kindness and curiosity. A smile, a nod, or a simple gesture can communicate volumes, often more effectively than words. And when you find yourself lost or uncertain, don't hesitate to ask for help. The Japanese people are renowned for their willingness to assist, often going out of their way to ensure you're on the right path.

As you reflect on your travels, consider the hidden gems that often lie just beyond the well-trodden paths. These are the places where the true spirit of Japan can be found, in the quiet corners of a bustling city or the untouched beauty of a rural landscape. Seek them out, for they hold the essence of what makes Japan so uniquely captivating.

In your quest to experience the "real" Japan, allow yourself to be open to serendipity. Some of the most memorable moments arise from unexpected encounters and spontaneous decisions. Whether it's stumbling upon a local festival, tasting an unfamiliar dish, or engaging in a conversation with a stranger, these serendipitous experiences often become the highlights of any journey.

As you prepare to leave Japan, take with you not just souvenirs, but a deeper understanding and appreciation of its culture and people. Let the lessons learned and the memories made inspire you long after you've returned home. Japan, with its rich tapestry of history, tradition, and innovation, will remain a part of you, a place to which you can always return in your heart and mind.

Finally, remember that travel is a lifelong journey. Each destination is a stepping stone, leading you to new adventures and discoveries. Let this guide be a starting point, a compass to navigate the wonders of Japan, and a reminder that the world is full of beauty and wonder, waiting to be explored. As you continue your travels, may you do so with an open heart and a curious spirit, ever ready to embrace the unknown.

• PERSONAL TRAVEL NOTES FROM OUR TOUR OF JAPAN IN THE YEAR 2022 AND 2024

As we sit down to reflect on our journey through Japan, it's hard not to feel a profound sense of gratitude for the experiences we've had and the people who have enriched our travels. The memories we've gathered are not just snapshots of beautiful landscapes or iconic landmarks but are deeply intertwined with the stories and warmth of the people we've met along the way.

Japan, with its vibrant cities and serene countryside, has a way of capturing the heart. From the bustling streets of Tokyo, where tradition meets the future in a dazzling dance, to the tranquil temples of Kyoto, where time seems to stand still, each place has left an indelible mark on us. We hope that through this guide, we've been able to share not just the practical tips for navigating this incredible country, but also the essence of its culture and the warmth of its people.

Our journey began in Tokyo, a city that never ceases to amaze. The energy of Shibuya Crossing, the serenity of the Meiji Shrine, and the quirky charm of Harajuku all offered a kaleidoscope of experiences. We were fortunate to have locals guide us through hidden gems, like a tiny izakaya tucked away in the backstreets of

Shinjuku, where we shared laughter and stories over sake and yakitori.

In Kyoto, we found a deep connection to Japan's history and traditions. Walking through the Arashiyama Bamboo Grove at dawn, we felt a sense of peace and wonder that words can barely capture. The hospitality of the ryokan owners, who welcomed us like family and shared tales of the past, made our stay truly unforgettable. It was here that we learned the art of the tea ceremony, a ritual that embodies the grace and mindfulness of Japanese culture.

Osaka, with its vibrant food scene and friendly locals, was a feast for the senses. The bustling Dotonbori district, with its neon lights and mouth-watering street food, was a highlight. We indulged in takoyaki and okonomiyaki, savoring each bite as we watched the world go by. The warmth and humor of the people we met in Osaka left us with a lasting impression of this lively city.

Beyond the well-trodden paths, we ventured into the countryside, where we discovered the hidden gems that truly make Japan special. In the small town of Takayama, nestled in the Japanese Alps, we were welcomed into a local festival, where we danced alongside the townspeople and marveled at the intricate floats parading through the streets. The beauty of the rural landscapes, with their terraced rice fields and traditional farmhouses, provided a serene backdrop to our adventures.

Throughout our travels, we were continually struck by the kindness and generosity of the Japanese people. From the shopkeeper in Nara who gifted us with handmade souvenirs to the elderly couple in Hiroshima who shared their personal stories of resilience, each encounter enriched our understanding of this remarkable country. Their stories and smiles reminded us of the importance of connection and the universal language of kindness.

We are deeply grateful to everyone who played a part in our journey. To the locals who welcomed us with open arms and shared their world with us, thank you for your hospitality and for making our trip so memorable. To our friends and family who supported us from afar, your encouragement and love have been a guiding light. And to our readers, thank you for joining us on this adventure. We hope that this guide serves as a gateway to your own unforgettable experiences in Japan.

As we conclude our personal notes, we carry with us the lessons learned and the friendships forged. Japan has taught us to embrace the present moment, to find beauty in simplicity, and to approach each day with curiosity and gratitude. These are the memories and lessons we hold dear, and we hope they inspire you as you embark on your own journey through the Land of the Rising Sun.

✓ Useful Numbers

When traveling to Japan, having essential phone numbers at your fingertips can be a lifesaver. From emergency services to tourist assistance, these numbers ensure you're prepared for any situation. Japan's unique emergency system differs from many countries, with separate numbers for police and medical emergencies. The Japan Visitor Hotline offers round-the-clock support in multiple languages, making it an invaluable resource for tourists. Knowing how to contact your embassy and use non-emergency services can also enhance your travel experience. Let's explore the crucial phone numbers you should have on hand for a safe and enjoyable visit to Japan.

Essential emergency numbers in Japan

In Japan, the emergency numbers are different from many other countries. It's crucial to memorize these numbers for quick access in case of an emergency:

- Police: 110 - Call this number to report crimes or accidents.
- Fire/Ambulance: 119 - Use this for medical emergencies or to report a fire.
- Coast Guard: 118 - Contact this number for emergencies at sea.

Remember that these services are available 24/7, 365 days a year. While English support is available, it's helpful to learn basic Japanese phrases like "Kaji desu" (There's a fire) or "Kyūkyū" (I need an ambulance) to expedite assistance.

229

For non-urgent medical advice, you can dial #7119. This service can help you determine whether you need an ambulance or can handle the situation yourself.

Japan Visitor Hotline: Your 24/7 support system

The Japan Visitor Hotline is an invaluable resource for tourists, operated by the Japan National Tourism Organization (JNTO). This service provides:

- 24/7 assistance in English, Chinese, and Korean
- Tourist information and guidance
- Help during emergencies, including accidents and natural disasters
- Support related to COVID-19 concerns

To reach the Japan Visitor Hotline, call 050-3816-2787 from within Japan, or +81-50-3816-2787 from overseas. This hotline can be a crucial lifeline, offering support and information when you need it most during your travels in Japan.

Embassy contact information for foreign visitors

Having your embassy's contact information is essential when traveling abroad. Here are some embassy numbers in Tokyo for major countries:

- United States: (03) 3224-5000
- United Kingdom: (03) 5211-1100
- Canada: (03) 5412-6200
- Australia: (03) 5232-4111

Remember to save your embassy's number in your phone before your trip. Your embassy can provide crucial assistance in emergencies, help with lost passports, or offer guidance on local laws and customs.

Important non-emergency numbers for tourists

While emergency numbers are crucial, there are several non-emergency numbers that can be useful during your stay in Japan:

- Japan Helpline: 0570-000-911 - A 24/7 service offering assistance in English for various non-emergency situations.
- Tourist Information Center: 03-3201-3331 - For general tourism inquiries (9 am - 5 pm).
- Lost and Found Center:
  - JR-EAST: 050-2016-1603 (10 am - 6 pm daily)
  - Tokyo Metro: 03-5227-5741 (9 am - 8 pm daily)
- Weatherphone: 177 - For weather forecasts in Japanese.

    These numbers can help you navigate common issues that may arise during your trip, from lost items to general inquiries about your travel in Japan.

How to make emergency calls in Japan

When making an emergency call in Japan, follow these steps:

1. Remain calm and speak clearly.
2. State the nature of your emergency (police, fire, or medical).
3. Provide your location as accurately as possible. Mention nearby landmarks if you're unsure of the exact address.
4. Describe the situation in detail.
5. Follow the operator's instructions and don't hang up until told to do so.

Remember, emergency calls are free from any phone, including public payphones. If using a mobile phone, you don't need to enter the area code before the emergency number.

> If you don't speak Japanese, say "Eigo ga hanasemasu ka?" (Do you speak English?) The operator will connect you to an interpreter if available.

Useful phone numbers for specific services

Here are some additional numbers that might be useful during your stay in Japan:

- Directory assistance: 104 - For looking up phone numbers (service in Japanese).
- Time announcement: 117 - To check the current time in Japan.
- TEPCO (Tokyo Electric Power Co.): 0120-995-002 - For power-related issues in Tokyo.
- Tokyo Gas (Gas Leak Emergency): 03-6735-8899
- Tokyo Waterworks Customer Service: 03-5326-1101 - For water-related issues.
- Tokyo English Life Line (TELL): 03-5774-0992 - For mental health support and counseling.
  Keep these numbers handy for specific situations you might encounter in cities like Tokyo, Osaka, or Kyoto.

Tips for staying connected and making calls in Japan

To ensure you can use these important numbers when needed, consider these tips for staying connected in Japan:

- Get a Japanese SIM card or pocket Wi-Fi for reliable internet access.

- Save important numbers in your phone and write them down as a backup.

- Learn basic Japanese phrases for emergencies.

- Download translation apps to assist with communication.

- Familiarize yourself with Japan's phone system:

  - Japan's country code is +81
  - Local numbers typically have 10 digits, including a 2-3 digit area code
  - When calling from abroad, drop the first 0 of the area code

Remember, staying connected is crucial for your safety and convenience during your trip to Japan. Whether you're exploring the bustling streets of Tokyo, the historic sites of Kyoto, or the vibrant atmosphere of Osaka, having these essential phone numbers and connectivity tips will ensure you're prepared for any situation that may arise during your Japanese adventure.

CALENDAR OF FESTIVALS AND TRADITIONAL EVENTS

Early February	Sapporo	**Sapporo Snow Festival:** Festival featuring spectacular snow and ice sculptures, events, and entertainment.
Early February	Kinosaki	**Oni Matsuri (Demon Festival):** Celebration featuring performances and dances to ward off evil spirits.
February	Sapporo	**Yuki Matsuri (Snow Festival):** Festival of snow and ice sculptures, with cultural events and activities.
March 3	All over Japan	**Hinamatsuri (Doll Festival):** Celebration for the health of girls, featuring displays of traditional dolls and family festivities.
March - April	All over Japan	**Hanami (Cherry Blossom Viewing):** Festival dedicated to viewing cherry blossoms in bloom, with picnics under the trees.
May (odd years)	Tokyo	**Kanda Matsuri:** Festival with processions of floats and rituals dedicated to the god Kanda.
May 1-3	Kyoto	**Kamo Matsuri:** Festival dedicated to the god of the Kamo River, featuring processions and rituals for good harvests.
May 15	Kyoto	**Aoi Matsuri (Hollyhock Festival):** Traditional festival featuring a historical procession in Heian-era costumes.
July	Kyoto	**Gion Matsuri (Gion Festival):** Famous festival for decorated floats and religious rituals celebrating the

god Yasaka.

Date	Location	Festival
July 1-15	Fukuoka	**Fukuoka Gion Yamakasa:** Festival known for its hand-pulled float races and lively celebrations.
July 7	Sendai	**Tanabata (Star Festival):** Celebration related to the legend of the stars, with colorful decorations and writing wishes on strips of paper.
July - August	Various	**Natsu Matsuri (Summer Festival):** Various summer celebrations characterized by dances, fireworks, and food stalls.
Last Saturday in July	Tokyo	**Sumida River Fireworks Festival:** Fireworks display on the Sumida River, one of the most famous fireworks festivals in Japan.
August	Aomori	**Aomori Nebuta Matsuri:** Festival featuring illuminated floats and dances, known for its spectacular lanterns.
August	Katsuura, Chiba	**Katsuura Fireworks Festival:** Fireworks festival along the coast, famous for its nighttime displays.
August 13-15	All over Japan	**Obon (Festival of Spirits):** Return of ancestors' spirits, with Bon Odori dances and commemorative ceremonies.
September 15 - October 17	Kyoto	**Kangetsu no Yube:** Kyoto Full Moon Viewing: Float on a boat in a pond under a clear autumn moon
October 7-9	Nagasaki	**Nagasaki Matsuri (Kunchi Matsuri):** Festival with Chinese influences, characterized by dances, processions, and a celebration of local culture.

October 12 - October 13	Kyoto	**Saiin Kasuga Shrine Festival:** A popular fall festival with parades, lantern displays, and food stalls
October 13	Kyoto	**Kyoto Intercollegiate Festa:** Organized by Kyoto students, featuring dance and music performances
October 21	Kyoto	**Traditional Noh Performance in Kyoto:** Experience Japan's dynamic traditional performing art
October 22	Kyoto	**Kurama Fire Festival:** A vibrant festival featuring bonfires, torches, shrines, and gods in the streets
October 22	Kyoto	**Jidai Matsuri (Festival of Eras):** A historical parade showcasing Kyoto's rich heritage for history buffs
April and October	Takayama	**Takayama Matsuri:** Festival with decorated floats and parades, celebrated in spring and autumn.
November 15	All over Japan	**Shichi-Go-San (Seven-Five-Three Festival):** Celebration for children aged seven, five, and three, who wear traditional clothing and visit shrines.

Regions and Prefectures of Japan

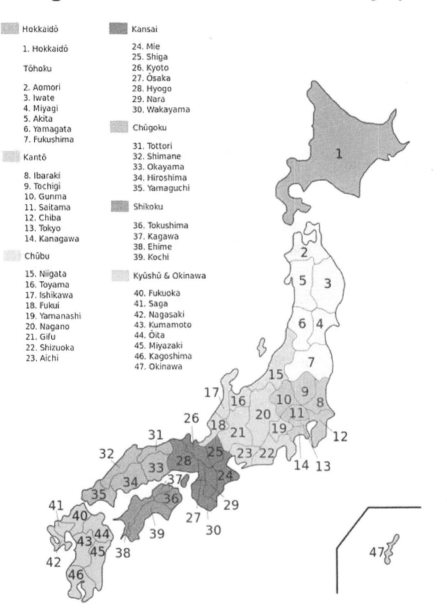

Hokkaidō

1. Hokkaidō

Tōhoku

2. Aomori
3. Iwate
4. Miyagi
5. Akita
6. Yamagata
7. Fukushima

Kantō

8. Ibaraki
9. Tochigi
10. Gunma
11. Saitama
12. Chiba
13. Tokyo
14. Kanagawa

Chūbu

15. Niigata
16. Toyama
17. Ishikawa
18. Fukui
19. Yamanashi
20. Nagano
21. Gifu
22. Shizuoka
23. Aichi

Kansai

24. Mie
25. Shiga
26. Kyoto
27. Ōsaka
28. Hyogo
29. Nara
30. Wakayama

Chūgoku

31. Tottori
32. Shimane
33. Okayama
34. Hiroshima
35. Yamaguchi

Shikoku

36. Tokushima
37. Kagawa
38. Ehime
39. Kochi

Kyūshū & Okinawa

40. Fukuoka
41. Saga
42. Nagasaki
43. Kumamoto
44. Ōita
45. Miyazaki
46. Kagoshima
47. Okinawa

Get Instant Access to Your

Free Bonus Now!

Scan me